S0-BHZ-914

HISTORIC PALESTINE, ISRAEL, AND THE EMERGING PALESTINIAN AUTONOMOUS AREAS

MIDDLE EAST

REGION IN TRANSITION

HISTORIC PALESTINE, ISRAEL, AND THE EMERGING PALESTINIAN AUTONOMOUS AREAS

EDITED BY LAURA S. ETHEREDGE, ASSOCIATE EDITOR, MIDDLE EAST GEOGRAPHY

Britannica Educational Publishing

IN ASSOCIATION WITH

ROSEN
EDUCATIONAL SERVICES

Published in 2011 by Britannica Educational Publishing
(a trademark of Encyclopædia Britannica, Inc.)
in association with Rosen Educational Services, LLC
29 East 21st Street, New York, NY 10010.

Copyright © 2011 Encyclopædia Britannica, Inc. Britannica, Encyclopædia Britannica, and the Thistle logo are registered trademarks of Encyclopædia Britannica, Inc. All rights reserved.

Rosen Educational Services materials copyright © 2011 Rosen Educational Services, LLC. All rights reserved.

Distributed exclusively by Rosen Educational Services.
For a listing of additional Britannica Educational Publishing titles, call toll free (800) 237-9932.

First Edition

Britannica Educational Publishing
Michael I. Levy: Executive Editor
J.E. Luebering: Senior Manager
Marilyn L. Barton: Senior Coordinator, Production Control
Steven Bosco: Director, Editorial Technologies
Lisa S. Braucher: Senior Producer and Data Editor
Yvette Charboneau: Senior Copy Editor
Kathy Nakamura: Manager, Media Acquisition
Laura S. Etheredge: Associate Editor, Middle East Geography

Rosen Educational Services
Jeanne Nagle: Senior Editor
Nelson Sá: Art Director
Cindy Reiman: Photography Manager
Nicole Russo: Designer
Matthew Cauli: Cover Design
Introduction by Laura Loria

Library of Congress Cataloging-in-Publication Data

Historic Palestine, Israel, and the emerging Palestinian autonomous areas edited by Laura S. Etheredge.— 1st ed.
    p. cm. — (Middle East: region in transition)
"In association with Britannica Educational Publishing, Rosen Educational Services."
Includes bibliographical references and index.
ISBN 978-1-61530-315-1 (library binding)
1. Palestine—History. 2. Palestine—Politics and government. 3. Palestine—Social conditions. 4. Israel—History. 5. Israel—Politics and government. 6. Israel—Social conditions. 7. West Bank—History. 8. West Bank—Politics and government. 9. West Bank—Social conditions. I. Etheredge, Laura.
DS117.H5515 2011
956.94—dc22

2010035792

Manufactured in the United States of America

On the cover (clockwise from top left): Israelis enjoy live music at a cafe bar in the centre of the northern Israeli city of Haifa, a view of Jerusalem, demonstrators in Jerusalem march in support of peace in the Gaza Strip, Palestinian men play cards at a cafe in the West Bank city of Hebron. *Menahem Kahana/AFP/Getty Images; © www.istockphoto.com/Oleg Babich; Shutterstock.com; Hazem Bader/AFP/Getty Images*

On pages 1, 70, 105, 123, 134, 145, 152, 209, 211, 218: An Israeli man and a Palestinian youth display their national flags. *Jack Guez/AFP/Getty Images (above); Hazem Bader/AFP/Getty Images (below)*

CONTENTS

INTRODUCTION

The history of the region known as Palestine, especially in the 20th and 21st centuries, has been marked by conflict. Over the last century, numerous governments, leaders, and organizations have grappled with the issue of how to accommodate the interests of both Israelis and Palestinian Arabs in the region. The Arab-Israeli conflict has had a ripple effect throughout the Middle East and has extended to the Western world as well. Allegiances have shifted, and alliances have been formed, broken, and re-formed numerous times. This book examines primarily the lengthy and storied history of a region treasured by three major faiths and explains how it has changed over the course of time.

The modern-day state of Israel is part of a region historically referred to as Palestine. The name is derived from the Greek term *Philistia*, which referred to the land of the Philistines, who occupied the territory in the 12th century BCE. The borders of the region itself are imprecise and variously defined. For the purposes of this volume, references to Palestine will refer generally to the area reaching from the Mediterranean Sea in the west to the Jordan River in the east, and from the Israeli-Lebanese border in the north narrowing down to the Gulf of Aqaba in the south.

The people of the Stone Age in historic Palestine were cave dwellers who increasingly turned to farming, eking out an existence on arid land. The earliest known towns, established in northern and central Palestine during the Early Bronze Age, were walled, mainly independent units. Egypt had some influence over the social and cultural development of the region until weakening Egyptian rule

A lithograph of the plan for Al-Aqsā Mosque and the Dome of the Rock, from an 18th century Arab manuscript. The latter is a sacred spot to both Jews and Muslims. The Bridgeman Art Library/Getty Images

in the region gave the Israelites the opportunity to occupy land east of the Jordan River as well as the western part of Palestine, near the end of the 13th century BCE. The Israelites established a temple from which the tenets of their monotheistic faith were spread.

According to biblical histories—which are the primary, yet frequently contested, source of information on the early days of the area—the Assyrians, Babylonians, and Persians each occupied ancient Palestine before it was conquered by Alexander the Great. For several generations, Palestine was the scene of many battles between the rival dynasties founded by Ptolemy I and Seleucus I, both of whom had served in Alexander's army and counted themselves his successors. Under the Ptolemies, it appears as though Palestinians in the southern portion of the territory retained a fair amount of autonomy, except for financial obligations to "tax farmers," individuals to whom the right to collect funds was granted or auctioned.

The Romans took over in the last century before the Common Era. King Herod of Judaea ruled Palestine during a period of peace and great economic success. After a brief period of divided rule predicated by familial infighting regarding who would be Herod's successor after his death in 4 BCE, Palestine then reverted to direct control by Rome's central government. A Jewish revolt led by Bar Kokhba in 135 CE was ruthlessly suppressed, and Jews were prohibited from entering Jerusalem and effectively eliminated in Judaea. Under Hadrian's rule, Jerusalem was made over into a true Greco-Roman city. With the conversion of Constantine I to Christianity in the 4th century CE, the newly Christianized area was inundated with pilgrims from various sectors of the Roman Empire.

Roman rule ended with Arab conquest of the region in the 7th century. Jerusalem became one of the holiest cities of Islam, while the population of Palestine as a whole shifted from Christian to Muslim and Arabic-speaking. The Jews began to return to the city in small numbers. For a brief interlude during the Crusades, Jerusalem was Christian territory but was quickly reclaimed by the Muslim Ayyūbid dynasty in 1244. Further Islamic conquests throughout Palestine ended with victory for the Mamlūks, who ruled prosperously for some 250 years. The Ottoman defeat of the Mamlūks in the early 16th century marked the beginning of an era of Ottoman dominance there that would last some four centuries.

The late 19th and early 20th centuries marked not only the development of Jewish agricultural settlement in Palestine, but also a broader Arab renaissance that touched the Palestinian population. Arab nationalism, and opposition to Zionism, became apparent in some segments of the intelligentsia even prior to World War I. Palestinian Arabs, by far the majority of the population, believed that British promises made during World War I included assurances of independence. Competing commitments made by the British to the Jews, as well as agreements reached with France and Russia, however, precluded this possibility. As political tensions rose, fighting broke out between the Arab and Jewish populations. In 1922 the League of Nations approved the British mandate over Palestine, and the 1917 Balfour Declaration—which had expressed British sympathy for the establishment of a Jewish national home in Palestine—was incorporated into its preamble.

Throughout the mandate period, the Jewish community strove to increase land holdings and immigration quotas, while Arabs sought to restrict both of these. This conflict of interest between the two factions periodically escalated into violence. In the 1930s, Jews fled

Europe as the Nazi Party rose to power. The effect on Palestine's population was staggering. By 1936, a full third of the population of Palestine was Jewish. The Arab revolt that began in 1936 prompted the British to launch an investigative commission, which in 1937 reported its findings that the mandate was unworkable. The rebellion continued until 1939, despite policing by the British. One consequence of the revolt was a strengthening and unification of the Zionists, a Jewish group who declared Palestine to be their homeland. In 1939 the British also issued a new White Paper that sought to limit Jewish immigration to a proposed Jewish national home that would be established in an independent Palestinian state. Both sides rejected it. Arabs mistrusted the British government, and Zionists were outraged by its failure to create a Jewish state.

During World War II, British efforts to restrict Jewish immigration led to attacks on British interests by Jewish militant elements. Meanwhile, the Arabs of Palestine showed their support of the Allies in the war; some even enlisted in their armies. After the war, when the atrocities of the Holocaust were fully known, pressure by the United States to create a Jewish homeland increased. Immigration continued to be a major source of conflict in the postwar period, and Zionist attacks continued, culminating in 1946 in an attack on Jerusalem's King David Hotel, an important British strategic centre, that cost 91 lives. Britain, exhausted of resources, turned Palestine over to the United Nations. In November 1947 the UN adopted Resolution 181, which stated that Palestine should be divided into two states, one Arab and one Jewish, which would retain economic interdependence. Jerusalem would come under international control. While the Zionists embraced the resolution, the

Arabs staunchly opposed it, and a civil war erupted. The British withdrew on May 14, 1948, and shortly thereafter the establishment of the state of Israel was proclaimed. Within hours it began to receive international recognition. War between the new state and its Arab neighbours erupted almost immediately, but by December 1948, the Arab armies had been soundly defeated.

Life for Palestinians—a term that has come to refer exclusively to Arab people of former mandate Palestine (excluding Israel)—was radically altered by the establishment of the state of Israel. Those who remained in Israel were citizens, but with restricted freedoms. Much of their land was confiscated, leaving many to abandon agriculture in favour of work as labourers. Jordan, which had taken control of the West Bank and East Jerusalem, extended citizenship to Arab Palestinians living in the West Bank. Those in the Gaza Strip were subjects of Egypt, which gave no offer of citizenship. Gaza was incredibly crowded. Many of its inhabitants lived in poverty and uncertainty, and a large proportion of Palestinians lived in refugee camps.

The events of 1948 and succeeding years helped forge a new generation's political and social identity, leading to the creation of several protest groups. Beginning in the 1960s, the Palestine Liberation Organization (PLO), an umbrella organization, established itself as the representative of the Palestinian cause and called for the liberation of Palestine and the obliteration of the state of Israel. The PLO entrenched itself in neighbouring Jordan, where it effectively operated as a state within a state. Tension between the PLO and the Jordanian establishment later came to a head in 1970, with the outbreak of civil war and the subsequent expulsion of the PLO from that country.

After the 1967 Six-Day War, which resulted in victory for Israel, more Palestinians fled the region. The annexation of additional land after the conflict, including the West Bank and Gaza Strip, meant that some three million Israelis came to rule just over one million Palestinians. Buoyed by the chance to reconnect with Palestinians residing in these locations, Arab Israelis started asserting their role in Israeli life, including participation in political and economic activity. The PLO gained international recognition and political clout; the organization's leader, Yāsir 'Arafāt, spoke before the UN in 1974. Israel's presence in the West Bank increased throughout the 1970s and '80s, and the PLO responded by strengthening its own presence there by providing services, including health care and education.

Israel had some conflicts with its neighbours, including Egypt. Unrest in the region, partly over disputed land claims, led to armed conflict between Egypt and Israel in 1969, which came to be known in Egypt as the War of Attrition. With Syria, Egypt also initiated a surprise assault on Israel in 1973 on the holy day of Yom Kippur. In 1977, U.S. Pres. Jimmy Carter facilitated the Camp David Accords, in which, among other provisions, Egypt and Israel agreed to a path toward self-governance for the West Bank and Gaza Strip. However, the Israeli government banned all anti-Zionist political parties, which effectively prohibited Palestinians from participating in Israel's political process. This contributed to the outbreak of the *intifāḍah* of 1987, a series of riots and demonstrations that lasted five years. In 1988, in the midst of this "shaking off," 'Arafāt proclaimed Palestine to be an independent state, albeit without defined borders.

The Gulf War of 1990-1 complicated matters in the Middle East. Israel held its fire against Iraq while allowing the U.S. to launch missiles from its terrain. After the war, and the fall of the Soviet Union, Israel and the PLO were ready to make a true effort toward peace. The Declaration of Principles on Palestinian Self-Rule, signed in September 1993 — the first of the documents that came to be known as the Oslo Accords — was a first step towards settlement of the matter. The agreement included a plan to transfer power over the West Bank and Gaza Strip to the Palestinians over five years, after which a permanent peace treaty would be negotiated. Israel began its pull-out the next year, and 'Arafāt was elected president of the Palestinian National Authority in 1996.

Israel began to shift toward granting autonomy to the Palestinian territories of the Gaza Strip and the West Bank. Yet promises on both sides were not kept, and by 2000 new uprisings threatened the already tenuous relationship between Israel and the Palestinians. Numerous setbacks — including increased Israeli settlement construction, continued attacks on Israelis by Palestinian militants, and the start of a second *intifādah* in 2000 — threatened efforts to reach a peaceful co-existence, although events such as Israel's removal of soldiers and settlers from parts of the West Bank and all of the Gaza Strip in 2005 periodically raised hopes for new peace talks.

Today, the West Bank and the Gaza Strip are under Palestinian control. 'Arafāt died in 2004 and was succeeded as president of the Palestinian National Authority by former prime minister Mahmoud Abbas. Legislative elections in 2006 brought further difficulties to the territories when the Ḥamās party unexpectedly defeated 'Arafāt's Fatah party. Clashes between the two followed, and in 2007 Abbas declared a state of emergency and dissolved the Ḥamās-led government. Since then, there has been an uneasy agreement that Ḥamās controls the Gaza

Strip while Fatah, which is recognized the world over as the leading Palestinian political authority, holds sway in the West Bank.

Israel, the sole Jewish state in the world, is a modern country. Ninety percent of its people live in cities, and citizens generally enjoy a high standard of living. Education is free and compulsory up to age 15, and universal health care and social services are accessible. Judaism is the predominant religion, although Islam is a distinct minority faith. Other religious minorities are free to practice their faiths as well. The country's economy, while robust, must support a large immigrant population and suffers from an unfavourable balance of trade.

It is uncertain whether the Arab-Israeli conflict will or can be resolved completely to everyone's satisfaction. There are numerous opinions about the state of the region, but no definitive answers. With new leaders, and old struggles, the Palestinian question, and the broader framework of the Arab-Israeli conflict, will undoubtedly continue to be explored in the future.

HISTORIC PALESTINE

The name "Palestine" has long been in popular use as a general term to denote a traditional region, but this usage does not imply precise boundaries. The perception of what constitutes Palestine's eastern boundary has been especially fluid, although the boundary frequently has been perceived as lying east of the Jordan River, extending at times to the edge of the Arabian Desert. In contemporary understanding, however, Palestine is generally defined as a region bounded on the east by the Jordan River, on the north by the border between modern Israel and Lebanon, on the west by the Mediterranean Sea (including the coast of Gaza), and on the south by the Negev, with its southernmost extension reaching the Gulf of Aqaba. The strategic importance of the area is immense. Through it pass the main roads from Egypt to Syria and from the Mediterranean to the hills beyond the Jordan River.

CHAPTER 1

A farmer harvests an orange grove located in Hod HaSharon, Israel. The Plain of Sharon has historically been fertile ground. David Silverman/ Getty Images

Coastal lowlands of varying widths front the Mediterranean. The most northerly is the Plain of 'Akko (Acre), which extends with a breadth of 5 to 9 miles (8 to 14 kilometre) for about 20 miles (32 km) from the Lebanon border in the north to the Carmel promontory, in Israel, in the south, where it narrows to a mere 600 feet (180 metres). Farther southward the lowland opens out rapidly into the Plain of Sharon, about 8 miles (13 km) wide and extending south to the latitude of Tel Aviv–Yafo. Once covered with marshes, the Sharon plain was reclaimed in the post-Exilic and Hellenistic period and is now a settled area. Fields and fruit groves are laid out between scattered sandstone ridges, on which villages have grown up. South of the spur of low hills that approaches the coast at about Yafo (Jaffa), the plain widens into a fertile region known in biblical times as Philistia, a district of orange groves, irrigated orchards, and fields of grain.

Farther northward the Plain of Esdraelon ('Emeq Yizre'el), formed by subsidence along lines of faults, separates the hills of southern Galilee from the mountains of Samaria. The plain, 16 miles (26 km) wide at most, narrows to the northwest, where the Qishon River breaks through to the Plain of 'Akko, and to the southeast, where the Harod River—which rises at the Spring of Harod—has carved the plain into the side of the Jordan Valley. Covered with rich basaltic soils washed down from the Galilean hills, Esdraelon is important both for its fertility and for the great highway it opens from the Mediterranean to the lands across the Jordan. The maritime plain connects with Esdraelon by the pass of Megiddo and several lesser routes between the mountain spurs of Carmel and Gilboa'.

The hill country of Galilee is better-watered and more thickly wooded than that of Samaria or Judaea. North of the Bet Netofa Valley (Plain of Asochis) is Upper Galilee, with elevations of 4,000 feet (1,200 m), a scrub-covered limestone plateau that is thinly populated. To the south, Lower Galilee—with its highest peak, Mount Tabor (1,929 feet [588 m])—is a land of east-west ridges enclosing sheltered vales like that of Nazareth, with rich basaltic soils.

Samaria, the region of the ancient kingdom of Israel, is a hilly district extending from the Plain of Esdraelon to the latitude of Ramallah. Its mountains—Carmel, Gilboaʻ, Aybāl (Ebal), and Al-Ṭūr (Gerizim)—are lower than those of Upper Galilee, while its basins, notably those of the ʻArrābah Plain and Nāblus, are wider and more gently contoured than their equivalents in Judaea. Samaria is easily approached from the coast across the Plain of Sharon and from the Jordan by the Fāriʻah valley. The city of Jerusalem has expanded rapidly along the mountain ridges.

From Ramallah in the north to Beersheba in the south, the high plateau of Judaea is a rocky wilderness of limestone, with rare patches of cultivation, as found around Al-Bīrah and Hebron. It is separated from the coastal plain by a longitudinal fosse and a belt of low hills of soft chalky limestone, about 5 to 8 miles (8 to 13 km) wide, known as Ha-Shefela. The Judaean plateau falls abruptly to the Jordan Valley, which is approached with difficulty along the wadis Kelt and Mukallik.

The Jordan Valley is a deep rift valley that varies in width from 1.5 to 14 miles (2.5 to 22 km). In its northern section the bed of the drained Lake Ḥula and of Lake Tiberias (the Sea of Galilee) are blocked by natural dams of basalt. Descending to about 1,310 feet (400 m) below sea level—the lowest land depth on the Earth's surface—the valley is exceedingly dry and hot, and cultivation is restricted to irrigated areas or rare oases, as at Jericho or at ʻEn Gedi by the shore of the Dead Sea.

The Negev, a desertlike region, is triangular in shape with the apex at the south. It extends from Beersheba in the north, where 8 inches (200 millimetres) or more of

precipitation falls annually and grain is grown, to the port
city of Elat on the Red Sea, in the extremely arid south.
It is bounded by the Sinai Peninsula on the west and the
northern extension of the Great Rift Valley on the east.

THE STONE AGE AND THE COPPER AGE

The Paleolithic Period (Old Stone Age) in Palestine was
first fully examined by the British archaeologist Dorothy
Garrod in her excavations of caves on the slopes of Mount
Carmel in 1929–34. The finds showed that at that stage
Palestine was culturally linked with Europe, and human
remains were recovered showing that the inhabitants were
of the same group as the Neanderthal inhabitants of
Europe. The Mesolithic Period (Middle Stone Age) is best
represented by a culture called Natufian, known from
excavations at ʿAin Mallāha and Jericho. The Natufians
lived in caves, as did their Paleolithic predecessors, but
there is a possibility that they were experimenting in agriculture, for the importance to them of the collection of
grain is shown by the artistic care that they lavished on
the carving of the hafts of their sickles and in the provision of utensils for grinding. During the subsequent
Neolithic Period (New Stone Age) humans gradually
undertook the domestication of animals, the cultivation
of crops, the production of pottery, and the building of
towns (e.g., Jericho by 7000 BCE).

Excavations also have provided a picture of events in
Palestine in the 5th–4th millennia BCE, during which the
transition from the Stone Age to the Copper Age took
place. It was probably in the 4th millennium that the
Ghassulians immigrated to Palestine. Their origin is not
known; they are called Ghassulians because the pottery

and flints characteristic of their settlements first attracted attention in the excavations of Tulaylāt al-Ghassūl in the Jordan Valley. There was a permanent village site with several successive layers of occupation, and the site probably was associated with reasonably efficient agriculture. The phase can be called the Aeneolithic or Chalcolithic Period or the Copper Age, since copper axes were found at Tulaylāt al-Ghassūl, and this is confirmed by the finds at sites near Beersheba, with pottery and a flint industry allied to those of Tulaylāt al-Ghassūl but not identical with them. At Beersheba there was a copper-working industry, which presumably imported ore from Sinai, and there was also evidence of an ivory-working industry, both proving the growth of a class of specialist craftsmen. Discoveries near 'En Gedi have revealed a shrine of that period, and basketry, ivory, leather, and hundreds of copper ritual objects were found in the Naḥal Mishmar caves of the Judaean desert.

The region in which the Ghassulian settlements have been found is mainly in the south of Palestine, with an extension up the coastal plain and its fringes. These settlements seem to have died out and disappeared in the last centuries of the 4th millennium, about the same time that a new population immigrated, probably from the north. Thereafter the composite elements in Palestine consisted of the indigenous Neolithic-Chalcolithic population, the Ghassulians, and these latest immigrants; in time the peoples were amalgamated into what was to become the sedentary urban population of the Early Bronze Age in the 3rd millennium.

Palestine's dating is henceforth linked to Egyptian dating until the time of the Hebrew monarchy. The interpretation of Egyptian dates in German Egyptologist Rolf Krauss's *Sothis- und Monddaten* (1985; "Sothic and Lunar Dates") is followed in this book.

THE BRONZE AGE

Most of the towns that are known in historic times came
into existence during the Early Bronze Age. The growth of
these towns can be approximately correlated chronologi-
cally with the development of the Old Kingdom in Egypt,
Early Bronze I corresponding to the late Predynastic
Period and Early Bronze II being cross-dated by finds to
the time of the 1st dynasty, c. 2925 BCE. Evidence of the
early phases of the Early Bronze Age comes mainly from
Megiddo, Jericho, Tall al-Far'ah, Tel Bet She'an, Khirbat
al-Karak, and Ai (Khirbat 'Ayy). All these sites are in
northern or central Palestine, and it was there that the
Early Bronze Age towns seem to have developed. The
towns of southern Palestine—for instance, Tel Lakhish,
Kiriath-sepher, and Tel Ḥasi—seem only to have been
established in Early Bronze III. The town dwellers, identified as the original Semitic population, can, for the sake
of convenience, be called Canaanites, although the term is
not attested before the middle of the 2nd millennium BCE.

In the course of the 3rd millennium BCE, therefore,
walled towns began to appear throughout Palestine. There
is no evidence that the next step of unification under the
leadership of a single town took place in the region, as it
had in Mesopotamia and Egypt; Palestine's towns presumably remained independent city-states, except insofar as
Egypt may at times have exercised a loose political control.
By about the 23rd century BCE the whole civilization had
ceased to be urban. During the next phase it was pastoral
and was influenced by the settlement of nomads probably from east of the Jordan River. Among the nomads,
Amorites from the Syrian Desert may have predominated.
It is not yet fully understood how these events are related
to the creation of the Akkadian empire in Mesopotamia
under Sargon of Akkad and his grandson Naram-Sin (24th

6

and 23rd centuries BCE) and to the latter's destruction of the powerful kingdom of Ebla (modern Tall Mardikh) in neighbouring Syria, nor is the extent of Eblaite and Akkadian hegemony over Palestine in this period known. It does seem reasonable, however, to associate the incursion of nomads from the east with the invasions of Egypt by people from Asia that brought the Old Kingdom to an end. An initial date of 23rd–22nd centuries BCE, depending on the interpretation of the Egyptian evidence, and a final date of the 20th century BCE seem probable.

The picture of Palestine at this period is thus unequivocally that of a region occupied by a number of allied tribes. Although they had many features in common, there were also many differences. The most significant point is that, with the possible exception of the northern group, they made no contribution at all to town life. The different groups had tribal centres, but they were essentially semi-nomadic pastoralists. This description fits well, given that in the Book of Joshua, the Amorites lived in the hill country, as opposed to the Canaanites, who lived in the plains and on the coast—areas favourable to agriculture.

It was, in fact, the next period—the Middle Bronze Age—that introduced the Canaanite culture as found by the Israelites on their entry into Palestine. The Middle Bronze Age (c. 2000–c. 1550 BCE) provides the background for the beginning of the story of the Hebrew Bible. The archaeological evidence for the period shows new types of pottery, weapons, and burial practices. Once more an urban civilization based on agriculture was established. It is not entirely clear whether the wave of urban development after the 20th century BCE was the work of a new immigrant people accustomed to town dwelling or of the local inhabitants themselves, some of whom may have adopted a sedentary lifestyle and begun, as in Mesopotamia and Syria, to establish dynasties. But where they settled, towns of the widespread Middle Bronze Age civilization of Palestine emerged. This civilization was intimately connected with that of the towns of the Phoenician-Canaanite coast. Extant Egyptian documents provide valuable information about Palestine in the period of the Egyptian 12th dynasty (1938–1756 BCE) and argue for significant Egyptian interest and influence in Palestine at this time. Most notable are the popular literary work known as the *Story of Sinuhe*, detailing the hero's exile in the Palestinian region, and the 20th–19th-century "Execration Texts," inscriptions of Egypt's enemies' names on pottery, which was ceremonially broken to invoke a curse. The culture introduced at this stage was essentially the same as the culture found by the Israelites who moved into Palestine in the 14th and 13th centuries BCE.

A large repertory of new forms in pottery arose, and for the first time in Palestine the clay was turned entirely on a fast wheel. Comparisons of Palestinian early Middle Bronze pottery forms with metallic and ceramic forms at Byblos, dated by Egyptian contacts, suggest that these forms were brought to Palestine about the 19th century from coastal Syria. Bronze weapons of a distinctive type, paralleled also on the Syrian coast, have been found at Megiddo, Jericho, and Tall al-ʿAjjul. Town life in Palestine gradually expanded after the mid-19th century BCE, but the material culture was essentially a direct development from the preceding stage.

Several towns of Middle Bronze Age Palestine were defended by plaster-faced ramparts (clearly discernible at Jericho and many other sites), an imported method of fortification giving evidence of a new and alien influence superimposed on the existing Canaanite culture. These were probably introduced by the Asiatic Hyksos, possibly related to the Amorites, who secured control of northern Egypt about 1630. The Hyksos may have included

8

elements of a grouping of people, largely Semitic, called the Habiru or Hapiru (Egyptian: "'Apiru"). The term *Habiru*, meaning "outsiders," was applied to nomads, fugitives, bandits, and workers of inferior status. The word is etymologically related to "Hebrew," and the relationship of the Habiru (and aforementioned Hyksos) to the Hebrews has long been debated. The Habiru appear to have established a military aristocracy in Palestine, bringing to the towns new defenses and new prosperity (as well as many Egyptian cultural elements) without interrupting the basic character of the local culture; this was to survive the destruction of Megiddo, Jericho, and Kiriath-sepher that followed the Egyptians' expulsion of the Hyksos into Palestine at the end of the Middle Bronze Age (*c.* 1550).

Sinuhe

(*fl. 20th century* BCE)

Sinuhe was the protagonist of a literary tale set in the early 12th dynasty (1938–1756 BCE) who fled Egypt to settle in Syria. His story yields information about political and social conditions of the time.

Sinuhe was an official of the harem maintained for Amenemhet I by his queen. While on an expedition to Libya, he learned of the king's assassination (1908 BCE) and fled, either out of fright or because of his complicity. He intended to travel southward but was diverted to the north while crossing the Nile River, and he passed into Palestine. After much wandering in Palestine and Lebanon, he was invited to settle with a chieftain of southern Syria, who adopted him and married him to his eldest daughter. In that land Sinuhe raised a family and became a veritable patriarch. He defended his father-in-law's territory and entertained emissaries traveling to and from Egypt.

The pharaoh Sesostris I invited Sinuhe to return to Egypt, and Sinuhe eagerly accepted. The king forgave him his real or imagined crimes and welcomed him with rich gifts; thereafter Sinuhe remarried in his homeland, while the pharaoh ordered a fine tomb built for him. Sinuhe's tale survived as a popular epic; internal evidence suggests that it is based on actual events. The story of Sinuhe was adapted by a 20th-century Finnish writer, Mika Waltari, for a popular novel, *The Egyptian* (1949).

There was no sharp break between the Middle and Late Bronze Age in Palestine. Shortly before the death of Ahmose I (1514 BCE), the first native pharaoh of the New Kingdom, the Egyptian armies began to conquer Palestine, probably completing their task during his successor's reign. Under Queen Hatshepsut (ruled 1479–58) Palestine revolted against Egyptian domination, but the rebellion was put down firmly by her successor, Thutmose III, who established a stable administration, maintained through the reigns of his immediate successors. Egyptian administrative documents excavated in both Egypt and Palestine show in considerable detail how the provincial government was organized and even how it operated during the century 1450–1350 BCE. Documents show, for example, that the land of Retenu (Syria-Palestine) was divided into three administrative districts, each under an Egyptian governor. The third district (Canaan) included all of Palestine from the Egyptian border to Byblos. This period is often known as the Amarna Age and is vividly illustrated by several hundred letters written in cuneiform script, found in Egypt at Tell el-Amarna, site of the capital of the "heretic king" Akhenaton. The unusual concern of the pharaohs with the affairs of Palestine was chiefly a result of the fact that control of it was necessary for the defense of Phoenicia and southern Syria, menaced by Mitanni until about 1375 and by the Hittite empire after that date.

About 1292 BCE the increasingly weak rule of the last pharaohs of the 18th dynasty was replaced by the strong arm of the second and third kings of the 19th dynasty, Seti I (ruled 1290–79 BCE) and Ramses II (ruled 1279–13 BCE). These kings blunted the southward thrust of the Hittites and consolidated the crumbling Egyptian empire. The exactions of foreign bureaucrats, however, combined with internal decay, had so enfeebled the Canaanite vassal princes of Palestine that it was comparatively easy for the incoming Israelites to occupy most of the hill country east of the Jordan River and in western Palestine during the closing decades of the 13th century BCE. Archaeological evidence suggests that the Israelite settlement in Palestine was much more complex and disconnected than the biblical accounts indicate. During a short interlude of anarchy that followed the last weak kings of the 19th dynasty, Egyptian rule was completely extinguished, and the ephemeral victories of Ramses III in the early decades of the 12th century scarcely affected Palestinian history.

Subsequent histories of the region have relied heavily on biblical narrative. Although this narrative has been augmented to a great extent by information derived from modern archaeological excavations — and, for some historical periods, by outside written sources — it is frequently the major, or sole, source of historical information; however, its validity has often been disputed.

THE IRON AGE

Though the Israelite tribes entered Palestine before the end of the Late Bronze Age, they did not become firmly established in their new home until the early decades of the 12th century BCE. The Israelites were overcome in subsequent centuries by the Assyrians, and in 612 BCE Nineveh, the Assyrian capital, was sacked by the Medes.

The former Assyrian empire was divided between Media
and Babylonia before the conquest of Media, Lydia, and
Babylonia by the Achaemenid dynasty brought the region
under Persian rule.

THE ISRAELITES IN PALESTINE

The Israelites' number was increased greatly during the settling of Canaan by seminomadic Hebrew tribes already in
Palestine, as well as by many settled Canaanites (e.g., the
Gibeonites), who joined the invaders against their sedentary
neighbours. Excavation has made it clear that the Israelites
began building amid the ruins of their precursors and that
new settlements sprang up rapidly all through the hill country. Had events followed their normal course, the resurgent
Canaanites, who had not been driven from the coastal plain
or the Plain of Esdraelon, might have overwhelmed the
scattered and unorganized Israelite clans, but this was prevented by the great invasion of the Sea Peoples in the time
of Ramses III, in the early decades of the 12th century BCE.

Among the invaders from the Aegean basin were the
Philistines, who were to conquer much of the region
within a century and a half after their settlement in the
southern coastal plain. (The Philistines have been identified with the so-called Peleset, who were used as garrison
troops and mercenaries by Ramses III.) Meanwhile, three
other peoples were settling east of the Jordan River: the
Edomites in the south, the Moabites east of the Dead Sea,
and the Ammonites on the edge of the Syrian Desert east
of Gilead. Considered by the Israelites as fellow Hebrews,
these peoples had begun to settle down before the Israelite
invasion, and they remained polytheists until the end of
the Old Testament period.

The early Israelites possessed a strong centralizing
force in their monotheistic faith, combined with a stern

code of ethics, which set them apart from all their neighbours. The Mosaic tradition of the covenant between Yahweh and Israel, made concrete by the Tabernacle and its ritual, bound the tribes together in a cultic bond resembling the later Greek amphictyonies. Characteristic of these organizations was a central sanctuary, surrounded by its worshipers. Straining against this religious bond were disruptive tribal forces held in leash by a loose alliance between the tribes, which was often severed by civil war. But for the constant attacks launched by its neighbours, Israel would perhaps never have attained any political solidarity. As it was, salvation from its foes lay only in union, and, after abortive attempts had been made at one-man rule, Saul became king of all of Israel (c. 1020 BCE).

Saul defeated the Ammonites and the Philistines but was killed in battle against the latter about 1000 BCE and was succeeded by David. King David crushed the Philistines (c. 990) and conquered the three Hebrew states east of the Jordan River, after which the intervention of the Aramaeans from Syria forced him to defeat and annex the states of Aram as far north as the borders of Hamath on the Orontes River. Farther east he established some sort of control over the nomadic tribes of the Syrian Desert as far as the Euphrates River, though it is scarcely probable that Israelite domination was that effective. At home David organized a stable administration based largely on Egyptian models and, according to tradition, carried out a census of the population. He died before he could complete his plans, but they were put into effect by his successor, Solomon.

The reign of Solomon (mid-10th century) represents the culmination of Israelite political history. Though Solomon gradually lost control over outlying territories conquered by David, he was extraordinarily successful in organizing the economic life of the country. He joined forces with

Hiram of Tyre, who was leading the Phoenicians toward the exploitation of Mediterranean trade. Expeditions to Ophir, a region probably in either East Africa or India, brought items of wealth such as gold, peacocks, and sandalwood to Palestine. At the same time, the Israelite king entered into trade relations with the Arabs as far south as Sheba, or Saba' (modern Yemen). These activities would have been impossible but for the development of new principles in shipbuilding and for the recent domestication of the Arabian camel and its use in the caravan trade.

Among the king's other undertakings was the construction of a fortress or storehouse at a site near the head of the Gulf of Aqaba. The modern site, Tell el-Kheleifah, may have been the biblical Ezion-geber. Most of the kingdom's wealth was spent in elaborate building operations, which included the Temple of Jerusalem and the royal palace, as well as numerous fortified towns. The best-known of these are Megiddo, Hazor, and Gezer. But royal activities on such a vast scale cost more than was produced by foreign trade and the tribute of vassal states, and the Israelites themselves were forced to submit to conscription in royal labour gangs as well as to heavy levies of various kinds. It is not surprising that the people of northern Israel revolted after the great king's death, thus disrupting the united monarchy.

The rump kingdom of Israel lasted two full centuries, sharing the worship of Yahweh and the Mosaic tradition with its smaller southern neighbour, Judah. After a period of intermittent warfare between Judah and Israel, King Asa of Judah entered into an alliance with the growing kingdom of Damascus, by which the latter attacked northern Israel, thus relieving pressure on Judah. This move cost Israel its territory to the east of the Jordan River and north of the Yarmūk River and ushered in a long series of wars between Israel and Damascus, which did not end until the capture of Damascus by the Assyrians in 732 BCE.

The ruins of the gate to the walled city of Megiddo. This fortified city was the site of many battles in historic Palestine. www.istockphoto.com / Elena Zapassky

The best-known phase of Israelite history is the period during which the great prophets, Elijah and Elisha, flourished, under the Omrides of the 9th century BCE. Omri himself, founder of the dynasty, selected Samaria as his capital and began constructing elaborate defenses and royal buildings, which have been uncovered by excavations. His son Ahab was alternately hero and villain of the principal stories of the prophets. He became involved in complex international maneuvers, which ended with his ignominious death at Ramoth-Gilead. The dynasty of Omri ended amid torrents of blood (c. 841 BCE); it was followed by the dynasty of Jehu, which lasted nearly a century. This was a period of extreme oscillations, from the catastrophic defeat of Israel (c. 815 BCE) and the destruction of its army by Hazael, king of Damascus, to the triumphs of Jeroboam II (ruled c. 786–746 BCE).

Meanwhile, Judah also oscillated between periods of prosperity and weakness. When it was strong, it controlled Edom and the caravan routes of the south from Midian to the Mediterranean; when it was feeble, it shrank behind its own narrow boundaries. Great kings such as Asa, Jehoshaphat, and Uzziah alternated with weak kings.

In 741/740 BCE the death knell of independence in Syria and Palestine was sounded by the capture of Arpad in northern Syria by the Assyrian king Tiglath-pileser III. Events unfolded with dizzying speed. In 738, Israel and Judah paid tribute to Assyria for the first time in decades. In 733, the Assyrians devastated Gilead and Galilee, turning the entire land into Assyrian provinces except for the territory of two tribes, western Manasseh and Ephraim. In 732, Damascus was captured and Aram ceased to exist as a state; and in 725 the siege of Samaria began. Finally, in the first months of 722, Samaria was taken and Israel became politically extinct.

ASSYRIAN AND BABYLONIAN RULE

Judah was left the sole heir of the legacy of David and Solomon. Hezekiah (ruled c. 715–c. 686 BCE), lured by promises of Egyptian aid, attempted to resist Assyria but was defeated and compelled to pay a crushing tribute. It is possible that only the timely intervention of an epidemic that decimated the Assyrian army of Sennacherib saved Judah from total devastation. The eloquent guidance of the prophet Isaiah restored the morale of the people, and even the weakness of Hezekiah's son Manasseh did not bring complete ruin. Another strong king, Josiah (ruled *c.* 640–609 BCE), arose in time to restore the ebbing fortunes of Judah for a few years, during which much of the ancient territory of united Israel was brought back under the rule of the Davidic dynasty. Assyria was rapidly declining in power, and in 612 its hated capital, Nineveh, was destroyed by the Medes. Josiah's successful rebellion ended when he fell in battle against a more powerful contender for the Assyrian succession, Necho of Egypt.

Meanwhile, the Chaldean kings of Babylonia were rapidly gaining strength. Nabopolassar of Babylon and Cyaxares of Media divided the old Assyrian empire between them, and the former's son, Nebuchadrezzar II, gained control of Syria and Palestine in swift campaigns. The defeated Egyptians, however, continued to intrigue in Palestine, whose native states repeatedly joined anti-Babylonian coalitions, all of which collapsed of themselves or were crushed by the Chaldean armies. Jerusalem was twice besieged, in 597 BCE and after 589 BCE. Finally, about 587/586 BCE, it was stormed and destroyed. The prophet Jeremiah, who had foreseen the tragic denouement and had repeatedly warned his people against their suicidal policy, died in Egypt. Judah was devastated and almost depopulated.

THE PERSIAN EMPIRE

In 539 BCE Cyrus II of the Persian Achaemenid dynasty followed up his triumph over Media by conquering Lydia and Babylonia, thus making himself ruler of the greatest empire thitherto known. In the administrative reforms implemented by Darius I (ruled 522–486 BCE), Phoenicia,

Palestine-Syria, and Cyprus constituted the fifth province (satrapy) of the Persian empire (Herodotus, *The History*, Book III, chapter 91).

One of Cyrus's first acts was to decree (*c.* 538 BCE) that Judah be restored and the Temple of Jerusalem be rebuilt. A large number of Jewish exiles in Babylonia returned to Jerusalem, and work on the Second Temple was begun. The political situation was extremely unfavourable, however, since Judah south of Hebron had been occupied by Edomites escaping from Arab pressure, while the tiny remainder north of Hebron had passed under the control of the governor of Samaria. In spite of political intrigues to prevent completion of the work of rebuilding the Temple, the Jews took advantage of the civil wars and rebellions that racked the empire after the accession of Darius I to press forward with the work. They were urged on by the fiery prophets Haggai and Zechariah. In 515 BCE the Second Temple was finished, but the Jews had meanwhile aroused the suspicion of the Persian authorities, and further efforts to improve their situation were discouraged.

Matters rested in this unsatisfactory state until about 445 BCE, when the Jewish royal favourite, Nehemiah, deeply stirred by reports of the sorry condition of Judah and Jerusalem, succeeded in obtaining the Persian ruler's support for a mission to Palestine. Under Nehemiah's leadership, Jerusalem's walls were rebuilt. Knowledge of the exact sequence of events is complicated by the confused state of the documentary sources, and the chronology of events in the time of Nehemiah and Ezra, who became a leader of the Jews who had returned to Jerusalem from Babylonia, is not certain. There is good evidence to suggest that Ezra's return to Jerusalem should be dated to 398 BCE, early in the reign of the Persian king Artaxerxes II. The mention of Persian intervention in the priestly affairs of the high priest Johanan can reasonably be associated with Ezra's reform activities. In any event, Nehemiah and Ezra were able to establish both the religious autonomy of Judah and the practice of normative Judaism so firmly that they continued with little change for several centuries.

Information concerning the history of Palestine in the period following the age of Nehemiah and Ezra is scanty. It is known that the province of Judah continued to be administered by high priests who struck their own coins and that the provinces of Samaria and Ammon remained under governors of the houses of Sanballat and Tobiah. In 343 Artaxerxes III (Ochus) is said to have devastated parts of Palestine in connection with his reconquest of Egypt. Eleven years later the country passed into Macedonian hands after Alexander the Great's conquest of Phoenicia.

FROM ALEXANDER THE GREAT TO 70 CE

To Alexander, Palestine was, as to many before him, a corridor leading to Egypt, the outlying Persian province. Consequently, in his attack on that province after the Battle of Issus (333 BCE), he confined his attention, in his passage southward, to reducing the coastal cities that might form bases for the Persian fleet. He left the Jews undisturbed in their religion and customs. The high priest remained the head of the Jewish state, perhaps assisted by a council of elders.

THE PTOLEMIES

After the death of Alexander in 323 BCE, Palestine, with much of Syria and Phoenicia, fell to Ptolemy I (Soter), who established himself as satrap in Egypt that same year and adopted the title of king by 304. (After the death of Ptolemy, the Ptolemaic dynasty ruled Egypt for 300 years.)

The successors of Alexander, including Ptolemy and Seleucus I (Nicator), defeated Antigonus I (Monophthalmus), another of Alexander's generals, who had almost succeeded in re-creating under his sole rule Alexander's vast empire, at the Battle of Ipsus in Phrygia in 301 BCE. This victory confirmed Ptolemy in his possession of his territory, although he had arrived too late for the battle, and Seleucus, whose participation in it had been decisive, at first disputed Ptolemy's claim to Syria and Phoenicia and actually occupied northern Syria. This early dispute laid the foundations of a century of bitter antagonism between the houses of Ptolemy and Seleucus that led to war five times—the so-called Syrian Wars—and was finally stilled only when Palestine, in 200 BCE, became part of the Seleucid kingdom. The northern boundary of the kingdom established by Ptolemy lay apparently slightly north of modern Tripoli, Lebanon, perhaps on the course of the Kabīr River (ancient Eleutherus), and there are no signs of any important change in this frontier throughout the next century.

PTOLEMY SOTER.

Portrait of Ptolemy I (Soter). Hulton Archive/Getty Images

Syrian Wars

The Syrian Wars (3rd century BCE) were five conflicts fought between the leading Hellenistic states, chiefly the Seleucid kingdom and Ptolemaic Egypt, and, in a lesser way, Macedonia. The complex and devious diplomacy that surrounded the wars was characteristic of the Hellenistic monarchies. The main issue in dispute between the Seleucids and the Ptolemies was control of southern Syria. In the First War (274–271) Ptolemy II wrested Phoenicia on the northern Syrian coast, most of Anatolia, and the Cyclades Islands from the Seleucids. In the Second War (c. 260–255/253) the Seleucid king Antiochus II, aided by Antigonus Gonatus of Macedonia, initiated a largely successful campaign to regain Phoenicia and Anatolia.

The Third, or Laodicean, War (c. 245–241) was begun by Ptolemy III to enforce earlier diplomatic arrangements disadvantageous to Seleucus II, son and successor of Antiochus II. To consolidate his position, Seleucus had to concede territory in Anatolia to the rulers of Cappadocia and Pontus. By the peace terms Ptolemy kept Seleucia Pieria in Syria and several coastal areas in Thrace.

In 236 Seleucus was forced to cede his Anatolian possessions to his brother Antiochus Hierax in the so-called War of the Brothers. Antiochus in turn lost them to the Anatolian ruler Attalus I of Pergamum. The former eastern Seleucid provinces, Bactria and Parthia, were also by this time in the hands of independent rulers. By 221 Antiochus III began to implement a policy of restoring Seleucid power, largely successful except for an abortive attack on Egypt.

In the Fourth War (219–217), which he initiated, Antiochus had to concede Coele Syria (southern Syria and Palestine) to Ptolemy IV, whose victory at Raphia in Palestine, however, was clouded by revolts in Egypt.

The Fifth War (202–200) climaxed a renewed and permanently successful Seleucid effort to wrest Coele Syria from the Ptolemies. Antiochus's subsequent Hellenizing policy in Judaea led to rebellion and independence for Judaea in 142. Weakened by constant warfare, the Hellenistic states fell under Roman control in the 2nd and 1st centuries BCE.

Of Ptolemaic rule in the southern part of this territory, Palestine, little is known. The small amount of information there is—mainly from writers of a later period, especially the author of the First Book of Maccabees and the Jewish historian Flavius Josephus—suggests that, unlike the northern region, known as Syria and Phoenicia, the area was left in much its previous state, with considerable power and authority in the hands of the native chieftains.

More is known of taxation than of administration. A story preserved by Josephus (*The Antiquities of the Jews*, Book XII, section 154 ff.) indicates that tax farming, whereby the right to collect taxes was auctioned or was awarded to privileged persons, was employed for the collection of local taxes. It seems likely that there were additional extraordinary taxes levied by edict from Egypt.

Knowledge of the economic and commercial life of Palestine in the mid-3rd century BCE is, on the other hand, fuller and more reliable. It is drawn from the dossier of letters received and written by one Zenon, the confidential business manager of the chief minister of Ptolemy II (Philadelphus; ruled 285–246 BCE). In 259 Zenon was sent to Palestine and Syria, where his master had commercial interests. His letters speak particularly of a trade in slaves, especially of young girls for prostitution, in whom there appears to have been a brisk commerce, with export to Egypt. Zenon's records also testify to a considerable trade in cereals, oil, and wine. Inevitably, like all imports to Egypt, Palestinian exports worked under state monopoly, without which the internal monopolies of Egypt would have been undermined. Palestine, like Egypt and Syria, seems to have had no economic freedom under Ptolemaic rule; in all transactions the hand of the government's agents is clearly visible.

Far less is known of the material culture of Palestine in the Ptolemaic period. The population seems, as in Syria, to have been divided between the Hellenized cities (*poleis*) of the coast, notably Ascalon (modern Ashqelon, Israel) and Joppa (Jaffa; part of modern Tel Aviv–Yafo), and the rural population living in villages (*komai*). The fact that several cities had Ptolemaic dynastic names (Philadelphia, Philoteria, Ptolemais) must not lead to the conclusion that the early Ptolemies wanted to urbanize and raise the standard of living of the people of Palestine. It seldom appears that they did more than rename a previously existing city (e.g., Scythopolis for Bet She'an)—a practice not uncommon in the Hellenistic world. In fact, unlike the Seleucids, the Ptolemies do not appear to have been great city builders. Nor do they appear to have encouraged the outward forms of independence in local government. It seems likely from the story of the Phoenician tax farmers mentioned above that considerable authority lay in the hands of the wealthy; yet the fact that both Ascalon and Joppa issued Ptolemaic regal coinage, but apparently no autonomous bronze coinage, suggests a rigid control. The absence of epigraphic evidence from the cities of Ptolemaic Palestine, however, renders any judgment about the conditions of the cities hazardous. Archaeology, too, helps but little, inasmuch as the buildings of Roman Palestine superseded most of the Hellenistic remains. One exception must be noted. The tombs of the Hellenized Sidonian military settlers at Marisa in Edom (Idumaea)—the walls of which are decorated with frescoes of fine hunting scenes—indicate that Hellenic civilization had been embraced by the non-Greek population in that period.

The chronic state of hostility between Ptolemaic Egypt and the Seleucid house, which in much of the 3rd century BCE had been concerned with the coastal regions of western Asia Minor, received a new impetus with the accession to the Seleucid throne of the energetic Antiochus III (the Great; ruled 223–187), who aimed to win southern Syria and

Palestine from Egypt, now weakly governed, and thereby establish the frontier to which Seleucus I had unwillingly renounced his claim in 301 BCE. After his decisive defeat by Ptolemy IV (Philopator) at Raphia in 217 BCE, however, Antiochus was for several years occupied with internal troubles, and it was therefore not until about 200 BCE that he could think again of an attack on Egypt. There a child—Ptolemy V (Epiphanes)—had recently ascended the throne, and the government was in the hands of overly powerful ministers who were more concerned with enriching themselves than with preserving the integrity of the kingdom. At Panion, on the northern boundary of Galilee, the armies of Antiochus and Ptolemy met, and Ptolemy was defeated. Thus the Ptolemaic possessions north of the Sinai desert, including Palestine, passed into the hands of the house of Seleucus.

THE SELEUCIDS

The Seleucids brought to the problem of the administration of Palestine a different tradition from that which had been behind Ptolemaic rule. The latter was based on the careful exploitation of territory that was possible in a small and closely knit land such as Egypt and had thence been extended to the Ptolemaic provinces. This had never been possible for the Seleucids, who had always been masters of regions so vast as to render a unified and absolute control impossible. There is no sign that the Seleucid government oppressed the native peoples—they seem, on the contrary, to have aimed at improving the natives' status as far as possible, largely through bringing them into contact with Greek modes of urban existence.

It might then be supposed that Seleucid rule would have been popular in Palestine. In fact, however, it was under Seleucid rule that the great uprising of the Jewish people, the revolt of the Maccabees, occurred. The explanation of this paradox is perhaps twofold. First, the Seleucids were in need of money, and, second, the throne, at a critical time, was occupied by a tactless and neurotic king. Knowledge of Seleucid rule in Palestine before the accession of Antiochus IV (Epiphanes; ruled 175–164 BCE) is slight. The period from 188 BCE onward was a lean time for the dynasty, because the war with Rome, which had ended (in 189 BCE) in a complete Roman victory, had cost it not only almost the whole of Asia Minor (Anatolia) but also a yearly indemnity of 15,000 talents. It is therefore not surprising that the first glimpse of Seleucid rule in Palestine tells of an attempt by Heliodorus, the leading minister of Seleucus IV (Philopator; ruled 187–175 BCE), to deprive the Second Temple in Jerusalem of its treasure. His failure was soon ascribed to divine protection.

With the accession of Antiochus Epiphanes, relations rapidly deteriorated. Antiochus appears to have aimed at a wholesale restoration of the Seleucid empire in the east, including an occupation of Egypt, as a counter to the loss of the western province occasioned by the Treaty of Apamea. He made an unwise beginning in Palestine by establishing a philhellene high priest, and it is clear from this and from his whole subsequent policy that he wished to extirpate Jewish religion from its central stronghold. (There is no indication that he persecuted Jews of the Diaspora [Greek: "Dispersion"] living in the cities of his kingdom.)

Antiochus invaded Egypt in 170 or 169 BCE, returning to Syria by way of Jerusalem, where he and his army despoiled the Temple of all its wealth. Two years later, after his humiliating expulsion from the gate of Egypt by the Roman legate, he sent a financial official to exact taxes from the cities of Judaea. Antiochus's official attacked the city of Jerusalem by guile and largely destroyed it. He then built a fortified position on the citadel, called by the Greeks the Akra. This became the symbol of Judah's enslavement, though in itself the presence of a royal garrison in a Hellenistic city was by no means unusual. Its imposition was followed by an open attack on religious practice, in which many rites were forbidden. Noncompliance with the order—which contained many items calculated to raise the bitterest resistance in the hearts of law-abiding Jews, such as the prohibition of circumcision and the abolition of the observance of the Sabbath—was punishable by death. Finally, on the 25th day of the Hebrew month Kislev (December) in 168 BCE, the "abomination of desolation," namely the altar of Zeus, was set up in the Temple in Jerusalem. It was this above all that summoned forth the resistance of the sons of the aged priest Mattathias; thus began the Maccabean revolt, led by Judas Maccabeus.

The resistance, it must be emphasized, came from only a section of the population. The century and a half of Greek rule had Hellenized much of the upper class of Jerusalem, and some of the characteristic features of Greek city life—such as the ephebic institute, for the training of young men, and the gymnasia—had been established on the initiative of this section of the ruling class, which was able to accept a less radical observance of Judaism and combine it with loyalty to the throne. Throughout the revolt, and indeed until the closing days of the Hasmonean dynasty established by the Maccabeans, this Hellenized element had to be taken into account.

Judas Maccabeus proved himself a leader of high quality. He successfully resisted the weak forces sent by the Seleucid authorities, and after three years of intermittent warfare he succeeded in purifying the Temple (165 BCE). The Akra, however, remained in Seleucid hands until 141 BCE.

After the death of Antiochus Epiphanes in 164 BCE, the numbers of claimants to the Seleucid throne made a continuous policy toward Palestine impossible, because each claimant felt the need to seek support wherever it might be found. Thus, Jewish high priests were bribed by the kings and dynasts of Syria. This development enabled Judas and those who succeeded him to hold their own and eventually to establish a hereditary dynasty, known as the Hasmonean for their ancestor Hasmoneus. Soon after Antiochus Epiphanes's death, an agreement was reached with the Seleucid regent Lysias (who feared the appearance of a rival in Syria) through which the Jews received back their religious liberty. But, at the same time, the regular practice of pagan worship, beside the Jewish, was established, and a Seleucid nominee was appointed high priest. Thus were laid the seeds of fresh revolt.

Almost immediately Judas again took the field and scored a considerable victory over Nicanor, the Seleucid general, in which the latter was killed. Within two months, however, Demetrius I (Soter), the Seleucid king, sent Bacchides to take up a position near Jerusalem, and, in the engagement that followed, Judas lost his life (161/160 BCE).

THE HASMONEAN PRIEST-PRINCES

In the following years, dynastic disputes within the Seleucid empire prevented a succession of rulers from settling the Palestinian question. These circumstances allowed first Jonathan (ruled 161/160–143/142 BCE), the brother and successor of Judas, and then his brother Simon (ruled 143/142–134 BCE) to attain power. In 153 BCE one of the Seleucid pretenders, Alexander Balas, in order to outplay the legitimate king, Demetrius, granted Jonathan the office of high priest and gave him the Seleucid rank of a courtier, thereby legitimizing his position. When Simon succeeded Jonathan, he acquired the status of a recognized secular ruler; the year he assumed rule was regarded as the first of a new era, and official documents were dated in his name and by his regnal year. He secured from the new Seleucid monarch, Demetrius II (Nicator; ruled 145–139 and 129–125 BCE), exemption from taxation for the Jews.

In 142–141 BCE Simon forced the Syrian garrison on the Akra to surrender, and the Jews passed a decree in his honour, granting the right of permanent incumbency to Simon and to his successors, until "an accredited prophet" should arise. It was thus in Simon's reign that the rule of the priest-prince was transformed into a secular heredi-tary rule. The Seleucid king recognized this, granting Simon the right to issue his own coins.

Simon's son, John Hyrcanus I (ruled 134–104 BCE), suffered an initial setback at the hands of the last great Seleucid king, Antiochus VII (Sidetes), who set out to reconquer Palestine, but at the latter's death John renewed his father's expansionist program, in which Samaria was conquered and destroyed. In internal pol-icy, however, he committed the grave error of quarreling with one of the two main Jewish ecclesiastical parties, the Pharisees—who followed the Law with great strictness and with whom the Maccabean movement had in origin close affinity—and siding with their opponents, the more liberal Sadducees. This is an early instance of that denial of the revolutionary origin of the movement that became entirely obvious in the reign of Alexander Jannaeus. Hyrcanus I was succeeded by Aristobulus I (ruled 104–103 BCE), who extended Hasmonean territory northward and is said to have assumed the title of king (*basileus*), though on his coins he appears, like Hyrcanus I, as high priest.

The reign of his brother and successor, Alexander Jannaeus, was long (ruled 103–76 BCE) and largely filled with wars. Alexander imposed his rule rigorously over an increasingly large area, including both the cities of the coast and the area east of the Jordan River. Still more clearly than Hyrcanus I, he attests the change in direction and aim of the Hasmonean house. He was the bitter enemy of the Pharisees, his coins bear Greek as well as Hebrew legends, and his title on them is simply "King Alexander." He was succeeded by his widow, Salome Alexandra, who reversed his policy and was guided by powerful religious advisers, members of the Pharisaic movement. After her death in 67 BCE her two sons Aristobulus II and Hyrcanus II fought for the succession. Hyrcanus was defeated but was encouraged to reassert his rights by Antipater, an Edomite, son of the governor of Idumaea and father of the future Herod the Great.

At that stage the Romans appeared on the scene. Pompey the Great, during his reorganization of the lands of the newly conquered Seleucid kingdom, also arranged the affairs of Palestine (63 BCE). He attempted to arbitrate between the brothers and eventually, after he had laid siege to and captured Jerusalem, appointed Hyrcanus II as high priest without the title of king adopted by his predecessors. He also imposed taxes on the Jews and curtailed Jewish dominions, granting virtual autonomy to a group of 10 or 11 Hellenized cities in Syria and Palestine, thenceforth to be known as the Decapolis, and placing them under the jurisdiction of the newly appointed governor of Syria. Pliny the Elder lists these cities as Damascus, Philadelphia (modern Amman, Jordan), Raphana, Scythopolis, Gadara, Hippos, Dion, Pella, Gerasa, and Canatha. On the basis of evidence in inscriptions, Abila can be added to the list. Thus, in spite of the name Decapolis, the actual number appears to have been 11. All these cities, except Scythopolis, are located east of the Jordan River, extending from Damascus in the north to Philadelphia in the south. Except for Damascus, all the other cities lie immediately to the east of Galilee, Samaria, or Judaea. Whether the Decapolis geographically belonged to Syria, to Coele Syria ("Hollow Syria"; i.e., the southernmost region of Syria, which may include Palestine and is sometimes mistakenly limited to the modern Bekaa valley), or to Arabia (often identified as the land east of the Jordan River) is not clear, especially in the ancient geographers. In any event, the Decapolis ended as a political entity when Rome annexed Arabia in 106 CE; the cities were distributed among the three provinces of Arabia, Judaea, and Syria. It appears that Philadelphia, Gerasa, and probably Dion went to Arabia, Damascus certainly to Syria, and the rest to Judaea or Syria.

After the death of Pompey, however, the power of Antipater and his family greatly increased. Hyrcanus II became a figurehead of no importance, and Antipater himself, in return for services to Julius Caesar, received Roman citizenship and was awarded the title of "procurator of Judaea," while his sons Phasael and Herod became governors (*strategoi*) of Jerusalem and Galilee, respectively. The unexpected occupation of Palestine by Parthian troops in 40 BCE altered the situation. Antigonus, the son of Aristobulus and therefore a legitimate Hasmonean, won the favour of the Parthians and was established by them as king and high priest of Jerusalem. Phasael was reported to have committed suicide, while his brother Herod escaped to Rome.

THE HERODIAN HOUSE AND THE ROMAN PROCURATORS

Herod, in Rome, was recognized by the Senate, with the approval of Octavian (later the emperor Caesar Augustus) and Mark Antony, as king of Judaea (40 BCE) and returned to Palestine in 39 BCE. Shortly afterward Roman troops expelled the Parthians, whose popularity in Palestine had been and subsequently remained considerable. After struggles against Antigonus, the Parthian nominee, in which he was assisted by Roman troops, Herod eventually captured Jerusalem. At about the same time, he married a niece of Antigonus, thus probably consoling those who remained loyal to the memory of the almost defunct Hasmonean house. Antigonus, when he fell into the hands of his enemies, was executed by order of Mark Antony.

The accession of Herod, a Roman protégé and an Edomite, brought to Palestine the peace that in the years of independence it had often lacked. His long reign (37–4 BCE) was marked by general prosperity; his new city of Caesarea (Caesarea Maritima) received lavish praise from Josephus for its spectacular port and extensive water and sewer system. Between 31 and 20 BCE, Augustus restored to him the Jewish territories that Pompey had taken away, and in this enlarged kingdom he created a sound administrative system of Hellenistic type. Toward the end of his life the complex demands of a vast family (he had at least nine wives) led him into difficulties regarding the succession, and it was then that he developed into the gruesome and vicious figure that Christian tradition has made so familiar. He had his wife Mariamne and several of his sons put to death to prevent them from succeeding him. On his death in 4 BCE the country again entered a period of divided rule, which led to the reestablishment of direct Roman government. Augustus decided later that year, in the presence of three surviving sons of Herod, that Herod Archelaus should rule Judaea, Samaria, and Edom (i.e., central and southern Palestine); Herod Antipas should rule Galilee and Peraea (east of the Jordan River); and Philip should rule Trachonitis, Batanaea, and Auranitis (the area between the Decapolis and Damascus).

The fates of these rulers (of whom Philip and Antipas were called tetrarchs, Archelaus ethnarch) and their territories were different. Philip, the most peaceable of the three, ruled the northern area until his death in 34 CE. Antipas reigned in Galilee and Peraea until 39 CE but was then banished by the emperor Caligula on the ground that he had parleyed with Rome's enemies. Archelaus reigned for 10 years only; he was removed at the request of his subjects in 6 CE. The region under Archelaus's rule (i.e., Judaea, Samaria, and Edom) became the province of Judaea and passed to a series of undistinguished Roman prefects, the last of whom (Pontius Pilate, ruled 26–36 CE) lost office for the unnecessary massacre of some Samaritans. Palestine finally was united under Caligula's protégé, Herod Agrippa I, who succeeded Philip in the north in 37 CE. The tetrarchy of Antipas was added soon after his removal in 39, and the territories of Judaea, Samaria, and Edom were added in 41, so that from 41 to his death in 44 Agrippa ruled the kingdom of his grandfather, Herod the Great, from Jerusalem. In 44 the entire kingdom passed under Roman rule and was reconstituted as the procuratorial province of Judaea.

Disturbances in the early years of procuratorial rule were frequent and caused largely by maladministration. Serious trouble arose under Ventidius Cumanus (ruled 48–52); and under his successor, the imperial freedman Felix (ruled 52–60), rebellion was open though sporadic. The incompetence and anti-Jewish posture of Gessius Florus, procurator 64–66, led in 66 to the decisive and final outbreak, known as the First Jewish Revolt. Florus, the heir to a long tradition of hostility between the large Hellenized populations of Palestine and the Jews (also a problem in the Diaspora, most notably at Alexandria during the reign of Caligula), allowed the Greek population of Caesarea Maritima to massacre the Jews of that city with impunity. Greeks in other towns of Palestine repeated the assault. In turn, the Jews responded by slaughtering Gentiles in Samaria, Galilee, and elsewhere. Soon Florus lost control of the situation. The organization of the Jews was better than it previously had been, and they were successful in an early engagement against the governor of Syria, who had advanced to Palestine with two legions to assist the hard-pressed procurator.

In 67, however, Vespasian, the future emperor, with his son Titus, arrived with a force of about 60,000 men, and the war became increasingly bitter. By the end of 67 Galilee was captured, and Judaea was reduced in three campaigns, which ended with the fall of Jerusalem in 70. The Temple was destroyed, though tradition recorded that Titus gave orders that it was to be spared, and the city became the permanent garrison town of a Roman legion. By 73 all resistance had ceased.

Events in Palestine during the first decades of the Christian era were of crucial importance to the development of Christianity as a world religion and to the re-creation of Judaism as a Diaspora community and the eventual establishment of Rabbinic Judaism as the normative expression of Jewish religious and cultural life.

ROMAN PALESTINE

After the destruction of Jerusalem, a legion (X Fretensis) was stationed on the site, and the rank of the provincial governor was raised from procurator to *legatus Augusti*, signifying a change from equestrian to senatorial rank. Caesarea Maritima, the governor's residence, became a Roman colony, and, as a reward for the loyalty of the Greeks in the revolt, a new pagan city, Neapolis (modern Nāblus in the West Bank), was founded at Shechem, the religious centre of the Samaritans.

The Jews, deprived of the Temple, founded a new religious centre in the rabbinical school of Jamnia (Jabneh). When a revolt broke out in 115 CE, the Roman emperor Trajan appointed the first consular legate of Judaea, Lucius Quietus, to suppress it. The rank of the legate confirms that two legions were stationed in Judaea, one at Jerusalem, the other at Caparcotna in Galilee, and thenceforth the province must have held consular status.

In 132 the emperor Hadrian decided to build a Roman colony, Aelia Capitolina, on the site of Jerusalem. The announcement of his plan, as well as his ban on circumcision (revoked later, but only for the Jews), provoked a much more serious uprising, the Second Jewish Revolt, led by Bar Kokhba. It was ruthlessly repressed by Julius Severus. According to certain accounts, almost 1,000 villages were destroyed and more than half a million people killed. In Judaea proper the Jews seem to have been virtually exterminated, but they survived in Galilee, which, like Samaria, appears to have held aloof from the revolt. Tiberias in Galilee became the seat of the Jewish patriarchs. The province of Judaea was renamed Syria Palaestina (later simply called Palaestina), and, according to Eusebius of Caeseria (*Ecclesiastical History*, Book IV, chapter 6), no Jew was thenceforth allowed to set foot in Jerusalem or the surrounding district. This prohibition apparently was relaxed sometime later to permit Jews to enter Jerusalem one day a year, on a day of mourning called Tisha be-Ava. Although this ban was officially still in force as late as the 4th century CE, there is some evidence that from the Severan period onward (after 193) Jews visited the city more frequently, especially at certain festival times, and even that there may have been some Jews in residence.

About the time the Bar Kokhba revolt was crushed (135), Hadrian proceeded to convert Jerusalem into a Greco-Roman city, with a circus, an amphitheatre, baths, and a theatre and with streets conforming to the Roman grid pattern. He also erected temples dedicated to Jupiter and himself (Aelia was his clan name) on the very site of the destroyed Temple of Jerusalem. To repopulate the city, Hadrian apparently brought in Greco-Syrians from the surrounding areas and even perhaps some legionary veterans. The urbanization and Hellenization of Palestine was continued during the reign of the emperor Septimius Severus (193–211 CE), except in Galilee, where the Jewish presence remained strong. New pagan cities were founded in Judaea at Eleutheropolis and Diospolis (formerly Lydda) and at Nicopolis (formerly Emmaus) under one of Severus's successors, Elagabalus (ruled 218–222). In addition, Severus issued a specific ban against Jewish proselytism.

After Constantine I converted to Christianity early in the 4th century, a new era of prosperity began for Palestine. The emperor himself built a magnificent church on the site of the Holy Sepulchre, the most sacred of Christian holy places; his mother, Saint Helena, built two others—at the place of the Nativity at Bethlehem and of the Ascension in Jerusalem—and his mother-in-law, Eutropia, built a church at Mamre. Palestine began to attract floods of pilgrims from all parts of the empire. It also became a great centre of the eremitic life (idiorrhythmic monasticism); men flocked from all quarters to become hermits in the Judaean wilderness, which was soon dotted with monasteries. Constantine added the southern half of Arabia to the province, but in 357–358 (or perhaps as late as the 390s) the addition was made a separate province under the name of Palaestina or Salutaris (later Palaestina Tertia). At the end of the 4th century, an enlarged Palestine was divided into three provinces: Prima, with its capital at Caesarea; Secunda, with its capital at Scythopolis (Bet She'an); and Salutaris, with its capital at Petra or possibly for a time at Elusa. It is clear that

the province of Palaestina underwent several territorial changes in the 4th century CE, but the details and
the chronology remain obscure. The governor of Prima
bore the high rank of proconsul from 382 to 385 and
again—as part of East Rome, which came to be known
as the Byzantine Empire after 476—from 535 onward. A
dux (Latin: "leader") of Palestine commanded the garrison of all three provinces.

The bishop of the civil capital, Caesarea, was, according to the usual rule, metropolitan of the province, but the
bishops of Jerusalem were claiming special prerogatives
as early as the first Council of Nicaea (325). Eventually,
Juvenal, bishop of Jerusalem from 421 to 458, achieved his
ambition and was recognized by the Council of Chalcedon
(451) as patriarch of the three provinces of Palestine.

There was a revolt of the Jews in Galilee in 352, which
was suppressed by Gallus Caesar. Under Marcian (ruled
450–457) and again under the Byzantine emperor Justinian
I (ruled 527–565), the Samaritans revolted. Palestine, like
Syria and Egypt, was also troubled by the Monophysite
controversy, a debate among Christians who disagreed
with the Council of Chalcedon's assertion that the person of Jesus Christ comprised two natures, human and
divine. When Juvenal returned from Chalcedon, having
signed the Council's canons, the monks of Palestine rose
and elected another bishop of Jerusalem, and military
force was required to subdue them. Gradually, however,
the Chalcedonian doctrine gained ground, and Palestine
became a stronghold of orthodoxy. Apart from these disturbances, the country enjoyed peace and prosperity until
611, when Khosrow II, king of Persia, launched an invasion of Byzantine territory. His troops captured Jerusalem
(614), destroyed churches, and carried off the True Cross.
In 628 the Byzantine emperor Heraclius recovered
Palestine, and he subsequently restored the True Cross to

Jerusalem, but 10 years later Arab armies invaded both the Persian and the Byzantine empires.

FROM THE ARAB CONQUEST TO 1900

The successful unification of the Arabian Peninsula under Islam by the first caliph, Abū Bakr (632–634), made it possible to channel the expansion of the Arab Muslims into new directions. Abū Bakr, therefore, summoned the faithful to a holy war (jihad) and quickly amassed a large army. He dispatched three detachments of about 3,000 (later increased to about 7,500) men each to start operations in southern and southeastern Syria. He died, however, before he could witness the results of these undertakings. The conquests he started were carried on by his successor, the caliph 'Umar I (634–644).

The first battle took place at Wadi Al-'Arabah, south of the Dead Sea. The Byzantine defenders were defeated and retreated toward Gaza but were overtaken and almost annihilated. In other places, however, the natural advantages of the defenders were more effective, and the invaders were hard-pressed. Khālid ibn al-Walīd, then operating in southern Iraq, was ordered to the aid of his fellow Arab generals on the Syrian front, and the combined forces won a bloody victory on July 30, 634, at a place in southern Palestine that the sources call Ajnādayn. All of Palestine then lay open to the invaders.

In the meantime, the emperor Heraclius was mustering his own large army and in 636 dispatched it against the Muslims. Khālid concentrated his troops on the Yarmūk River, the eastern tributary of the Jordan River. The decisive battle that delivered Palestine to the Muslims took place on Aug. 20, 636. Only Jerusalem and Caesarea held out, the former until 638, when it surrendered to the Muslims, and the latter until October 640. Palestine, and indeed all of Syria, was then in Muslim hands. After the surrender of Jerusalem, 'Umar divided Palestine into two administrative districts (*jund*) similar to the Roman and Byzantine provinces: they were Jordan (Al-Urdunn) and Palestine (Filasṭīn). Jordan included Galilee and Acre (modern 'Akko, Israel) and extended east to the desert; Palestine, with its capital first at Lydda (modern Lod, Israel) and later at Ramla (after 716), covered the region south of the Plain of Esdraelon.

'Umar lost no time in emphasizing Islam's interest in the holy city of Jerusalem as the first *qiblah*, the direction toward which, until 623, Muslims had turned their faces in prayer and as the third holiest spot in Islam. (The Prophet Muhammad himself had changed the *qiblah* to Mecca in 623.) On visiting the Temple Mount area—which Muslims came to know as Al-Ḥaram al-Sharīf (Arabic: "The Noble Sanctuary")—and finding the place suffering from neglect, 'Umar and his followers cleaned it with their own hands and declared it a sacred place of prayer, erecting there the first structure called Al-Aqṣā Mosque.

Dome of the Rock

The Dome of the Rock (Arabic: Qubbat al-Ṣakhrah) is a shrine in Jerusalem that is the oldest extant Islamic monument. The rock over which the shrine was built is sacred to both Muslims and Jews. The Prophet Muhammad, founder of Islam, is traditionally believed to have ascended into heaven from the site. In Jewish tradition, it is here that Abraham, the progenitor and first patriarch of the Hebrew people, is said to have prepared to sacrifice his son Isaac. The Dome and Al-Aqṣā Mosque are both located on the Temple Mount, the site of Solomon's Temple and its successors.

The original purpose of the Dome of the Rock, which was built between 685 and 691 CE by the caliph 'Abd al-Malik ibn Marwān,

Dome of the Rock, Jerusalem. Michael Freeman—Digital Vision/Getty Images

remains a source of debate. An unprecedented structure, it is virtually the first monumental building in Islamic history and is of considerable aesthetic and architectural importance; it is rich with mosaic, faience, and marble, much of which was added several centuries after its completion. Basically octagonal, the Dome of the Rock makes use of Byzantine techniques but is already distinctly Islamic. A wooden dome—approximately 60 feet (18 m) in diameter and mounted on an elevated drum—rises above a circle of 16 piers and columns. Surrounding this circle is an octagonal arcade of 24 piers and columns. The outer walls repeat this octagon, each of the eight sides being approximately 60 feet (18 m) wide and 36 feet (11 m) high. Both the dome and the exterior walls contain many windows.

Christians and Muslims in the Middle Ages believed the Dome itself to be the Temple of Solomon (Templum Domini). The Knights Templar were quartered there in the Crusades, and Templar churches in Europe imitated its plan.

UMAYYAD RULE

Under the Umayyads, a Muslim dynasty that gained power in 661 from the Meccans and Medinans who had initially led the Islamic community, Palestine formed, with Syria, one of the main provinces of the empire. Each *jund* was administered by an emir assisted by a financial officer. This pattern continued, in general, until the time of Ottoman rule.

For various reasons, the Umayyads paid special attention to Palestine. The process of Arabization and Islamization was gaining momentum there. It was one of the mainstays of Umayyad power and was important in their struggle against both Iraq and the Arabian Peninsula. The caliph 'Abd al-Malik (ruled 685–705) erected the Dome of the Rock between 685 and 691 on the site of the Temple of Solomon, which the Muslims believed had been the site of the Prophet's ascension into heaven. This magnificent structure represents the earliest Muslim monument still extant. Close to the shrine and to the south, 'Abd al-Malik's son, al-Walīd I (ruled 705–715), rebuilt Al-Aqṣā Mosque on a larger scale. The Umayyad caliph 'Umar II (ruled 717–720) imposed humiliating restrictions on his non-Muslim subjects, particularly the Christians. Conversions arising from convenience as well as conviction then increased. These conversions to Islam, together with a steady tribal inflow from the desert, changed the religious character of Palestine's inhabitants. The predominantly Christian population gradually became predominantly Muslim and Arabic-speaking. At the same time, during the early years of Muslim control of the city, a small permanent Jewish population returned to Jerusalem after a 500-year absence.

'ABBĀSID RULE

Umayyad rule ended in 750. Along with Syria, Palestine became subject to 'Abbāsid authority, based in Baghdad, and, like Syria, it did not readily submit to its new masters. Unlike the Umayyads, who leaned on the Yemeni (South Arabian) tribes, the 'Abbāsids, in Syria, favoured and indeed used the Qays (North Arabian) tribes. Enmity between the two groups was, therefore, intensified and became an important political factor in Palestine. Pro-Umayyad uprisings were frequent and received Palestinian support. In 840/841 Abū Ḥarb, a Yemenite, unfurled the white banner of the Umayyads and succeeded in recruiting a large number of peasant followers, mainly among the Palestinian population, who regarded him as the saviour whose appearance was to save the land from the hated 'Abbāsids. Though the insurrection was put down, unrest persisted.

The process of Islamization gained momentum under the 'Abbāsids. 'Abbāsid rulers encouraged the settlement and fortification of coastal Palestine so as to secure it against the Byzantine enemy. During the second half of the 9th century, however, signs of internal decay began to appear in the 'Abbāsid empire. Petty states, and some indeed not so petty, emerged in different parts of the realm. One of the first to affect Palestine was the Tūlūnid dynasty (868–905) of Egypt, which marked the beginning of the disengagement of Egypt and, with it, of Syria and Palestine from 'Abbāsid rule. During that period Palestine also experienced the destructive operations of the Qarmaṭians, an Ismā'īlī Shī'ite sect that launched an insurrection in 903–906. After 'Abbāsid authority was briefly restored, Palestine came under Ikhshīdid rule (935–969).

THE FĀṬIMID DYNASTY

In the meantime, the Shīʿite Fāṭimid dynasty was rising to power in North Africa. It moved eastward to seize not only Egypt but also Palestine and Syria and to threaten Baghdad itself. The Fāṭimids seized Egypt from the Ikhshīdids in 969 and in less than a decade were able to establish a precarious control over Palestine, where they faced Qarmaṭian, Seljuq, Byzantine, and periodic Bedouin opposition. Palestine was thus often reduced to a battlefield. The country suffered even greater hardship, however, under the Fāṭimid caliph al-Ḥākim (ruled 996–1021), whose behaviour was at times erratic and extremely harsh, particularly toward his non-Muslim subjects. He reactivated earlier discriminatory laws imposed on Christians and Jews and added new ones. In 1009 he ordered the destruction of the Church of the Holy Sepulchre, which was severely damaged as a result.

In 1071 the Seljuqs captured Jerusalem, which prospered as pilgrimages by Jews, Christians, and Muslims increased in spite of political instability. The Fāṭimids recaptured the city in 1098 only to relinquish it a year later to a new enemy, the Crusaders of western Europe.

THE CRUSADES

A year after the capture of Jerusalem by the Crusaders, the Latin kingdom of Jerusalem was established (Dec. 25, 1100). Thereafter there was no effective check to the expansion of the Crusaders' power until the capture of their stronghold at Edessa (modern Şanlıurfa, Tur.) by the *atabeg* (governor) of Mosul, ʿImād al-Dīn Zangī ibn Aq Sonqur, in 1144. Zangī's anti-Crusader campaign was carried on after his death by his son Nūr al-Dīn (Nureddin) and, more effectively, by the sultan Ṣalāḥ al-Dīn Yūsuf ibn Ayyūb (commonly known in the West as Saladin), a protégé of the *atabeg*'s family. After consolidating his position in Egypt and Syria, Saladin waged relentless war against the "infidel" Franks (Western Christians). On July 4, 1187, six days after the capture of Tiberias, he dealt the Crusaders a crushing blow at the decisive Battle of Ḥaṭṭīn (Ḥiṭṭīn). Most of Palestine was once again Muslim. Further attempts by the Crusaders to regain control of Palestine proved ineffective, primarily because of incessant quarrels among the Crusaders themselves. Ironically, it was left to an emperor of dubious Christian standing, Frederick II, to negotiate in 1229, while under excommunication, a 10-year treaty that temporarily restored Jerusalem, Nazareth, and Bethlehem to the Christians. In 1244, however, the Ayyūbid sultan al-Ṣāliḥ Ayyūb definitively restored Jerusalem to Islam.

While the Ayyūbids of Saladin's house were losing ground to the Turkish-speaking Mamlūks in Egypt, the Mongol sweep westward continued, placing the Crusaders, as it were, between two fires. To make matters worse, the Crusaders themselves were hopelessly riddled with dissension. In 1260 the Mamlūk leader Baybars I emerged as a champion of Muslim resurgence. After taking part in the defeat of the Mongols at the Battle of 'Ayn Jālūt in Palestine, he murdered the incumbent sultan and seized the throne; in the years 1263 to 1271 he carried out annual raids against the harassed Franks. His efforts were continued by the sultan al-Ashraf Ṣalāḥ al-Dīn Khalīl, during whose reign the last of the Crusaders were driven out of Acre (May 18, 1291). A chapter in the history of Palestine thus came to an end. The Mamlūks and subsequent Muslim regimes ruled the area with only brief interruptions for the next 600 years.

Palestine under the Mamlūks in the 14th century saw a period of prosperity for some; this was especially notable in Jerusalem, where the government sponsored an elaborate program to construct schools, establish lodgings for travelers and Muslim pilgrims, and renovate mosques. Tax revenues, collected mainly from the villages, were spent largely on support of religious institutions. Palestine formed a part of the district of Damascus, second only to Egypt in the Mamlūk domains. The region suffered the ravages of several epidemics, including the great pestilence, the same Black Death that in 1347–51 devastated Europe.

The fall of the Baḥrī Mamlūks and the rise of the Burjī Mamlūks (1382–1517) contributed to a gradual economic deterioration and a decrease in security. During the reigns of the second Burjī sultan, Faraj (1399–1405 and 1405–12), the last onslaught of the Mongols, which made the name of Timur (Tamerlane) a synonym of destruction and plunder, took place. Although Palestine was spared the pillage of his hordes, it could not escape its disastrous repercussions as the Mamlūks moved through in a vain attempt to defend Damascus against the invader. The death of Timur in 1405, and the weakness of Iran in the ensuing century, pitted the Mamlūks against the rising power of the Ottoman Empire for the control of western Asia. Hostilities broke out in 1486 when Sultan Qā'it Bāy contested with Bayezid II the possession of some border towns. The climax came three decades later on Aug. 24, 1516, when the Ottoman sultan, Selim I, routed the Mamlūk armies at the Battle of Marj Dābiq. Palestine began its four centuries under Ottoman domination.

OTTOMAN RULE

Under the Ottoman Turks, Palestine continued to be linked administratively to Damascus until 1830, when it was placed under Sidon, then under Acre, then once again under Damascus until 1887–88, at which time the administrative divisions of the Ottoman Empire were settled for the last time. Palestine was divided into the districts of Nāblus and Acre, both of which were linked with the province of Beirut and the autonomous district of Jerusalem, which dealt directly with Istanbul. With varying fortunes often accompanied by revolts, massacres, and wars, the first three centuries of Ottoman rule isolated Palestine from most outside influences. The prosperity of 16th-century Ottoman Palestine was followed by an economic and political decline in the 17th century. Ottoman control in the 18th century was indirect. Ḍāhir al-ʿUmar (ruled *c.* 1737–75) dominated the political life of northern Palestine for nearly 40 years. Aḥmad al-Jazzār, the Ottoman governor of Acre, had control of most of Palestine, and in 1799, with English and Ottoman help, he successfully defended Acre against Napoleon I.

Both Ḍāhir and al-Jazzār presided over a tightly controlled Palestine, where trade with Europe as well as taxation were growing. They used their new wealth from these sources to gain influence in Istanbul, which allowed them to gain local autonomy and even intermittent control of many areas outside Palestine.

This period came to an end with Napoleon's abortive attempt (1798–1801) to carve for himself a Middle Eastern empire. Egypt, always a determining factor in the fortunes of Palestine, was placed, after the French withdrawal, under the rule of the viceroy Muḥammad ʿAlī, who soon embarked on a program of expansion at the expense of his Ottoman overlord. In 1831 his armies occupied Palestine, and for nine years he and his son Ibrāhīm gave it a centralizing and modernizing administration. Their rule increasingly opened the country to Western influences and enabled Christian missionaries to establish many schools. At the same time, however, taxes were increased, and urban rebellions broke out against the harshness of the regime. When in 1840 the British, the Austrians, and the

Russians came to the aid of the Ottomans, the Egyptians were forced to withdraw, and Palestine reverted to the Ottoman Empire. Increased European interest, however, led the powers to establish consulates in Jerusalem and in Palestine's port cities.

After 1840 the reforms the sultan promulgated gradually took effect in Palestine. Increased security in the countryside and the Ottoman Land Law of 1858 encouraged the development of private property, agricultural production for the world market, the decline of tribal social organization, growth of the population, and the enrichment of the notable families. As the Ottomans extended the central government's new military, municipal, judicial, and educational systems to Palestine, the country also witnessed a marked increase in foreign settlements and colonies—French, Russian, and German. By far the most important, in spite of their initial numerical insignificance, were the Jewish agricultural settlements, which foreshadowed later Zionist endeavours to establish a Jewish national home and still later a Jewish state (Israel) in Palestine. The earliest of these settlements was founded by Russian Jews in 1882. In 1896 Theodor Herzl issued a pamphlet entitled *Der Judenstaat* (*The Jewish State*) and advocated an autonomous Jewish state, preferably in Palestine. Two years later he himself went to Palestine to investigate its possibilities and, possibly, to seek the help of the German emperor William II, who was then making a spectacular pilgrimage to the Holy Land.

FROM 1900 TO 1948

In the last years of the 19th century and the early years of the 20th, the Palestinian Arabs shared in a general Arab renaissance. Palestinians found opportunities in the service of the Ottoman Empire, and Palestinian deputies sat in the Ottoman parliaments of 1877, 1908, 1912, and 1914. Several Arabic newspapers appeared in the country before 1914. Their pages reveal that Arab nationalism and opposition to Zionism were strong among some sections of the intelligentsia even before World War I. The Arabs sought an end to Jewish immigration and to land purchases by Zionists. The number of Zionist colonies, however, mostly subsidized by the French philanthropist Edmond, baron de Rothschild, rose from 19 in 1900 to 47 in 1918, even though the majority of the Jews were town dwellers. The population of Palestine, predominantly agricultural, was about 690,000 in 1914 (535,000 Muslims; 70,000 Christians, most of whom were Arabs; and 85,000 Jews).

WORLD WAR I AND AFTER

During World War I the great powers made a number of decisions concerning the future of Palestine without much regard to the wishes of the indigenous inhabitants. Palestinian Arabs, however, believed that Great Britain had promised them independence in the Ḥusayn-McMahon correspondence, an exchange of letters from July 1915 to March 1916 between Sir Henry McMahon, British high commissioner in Egypt, and Ḥusayn ibn 'Alī, then emir of Mecca, in which the British made certain commitments to the Arabs in return for their support against the Ottomans during the war. Yet by May 1916 Great Britain, France, and Russia had reached an agreement (the Sykes-Picot Agreement) according to which, inter alia, the bulk of Palestine was to be internationalized. Further complicating the situation, in November 1917 Arthur Balfour, the British secretary of state for foreign affairs, addressed a letter to Lord Lionel Walter Rothschild (the Balfour Declaration) expressing sympathy for the establishment in Palestine of a national home for the Jewish people on the understanding that "nothing shall be done which may prejudice the civil and religious rights of existing non-Jewish communities in Palestine." This declaration did not come about through an act of generosity or stirrings of conscience over the bitter fate of the Jewish people. It was meant, in part, to prompt American Jews to exercise their influence in moving the United States to support British postwar policies as well as to encourage Russian Jews to keep their country fighting.

Sykes-Picot Agreement

The Sykes-Picot Agreement (May 9, 1916) was a secret convention made during World War I between Great Britain and France, with the assent of imperial Russia, for the dismemberment of the Ottoman Empire. The agreement led to the division of Turkish-held Syria, Iraq, Lebanon, and Palestine into various French- and British-administered areas. The agreement took its name from its negotiators, Sir Mark Sykes of Britain and François Georges-Picot of France.

Its provisions were as follows: (1) Russia should acquire the Armenian provinces of Erzurum, Trebizond (Trabzon), Van, and Bitlis, with some Kurdish territory to the southeast; (2) France should acquire Lebanon and the Syrian littoral, Adana, Cilicia, and the hinterland adjacent to Russia's share, that hinterland including Aintab, Urfa, Mardin, Diyarbakır, and Mosul; (3) Great Britain should acquire southern Mesopotamia, including Baghdad, and also the Mediterranean ports of Haifa and 'Akko (Acre); (4) between the French and the British acquisitions there should be a confederation of Arab states or a single independent Arab state, divided into French and British spheres of influence; (5) Alexandretta (Iskenderun) should be a free port; and (6) Palestine, because of the holy places, should be under an international regime.

This secret arrangement conflicted in the first place with pledges already given by the British to the Hāshimite dynast Ḥusayn ibn 'Alī, emir of Mecca, who was about to bring the Arabs of the Hejaz into revolt against the Turks on the understanding that the Arabs would eventually receive a much more important share of the fruits of victory. It also excited the ambitions of Italy, to whom it was communicated in August 1916, after the Italian declaration of war against Germany, with the result that it had to be supplemented, in April 1917, by the Agreement of Saint-Jean-de-Maurienne, whereby Great Britain and France promised southern and southwestern Anatolia to Italy. The defection of Russia from the war canceled the Russian aspect of the Sykes-Picot Agreement; and the Turkish Nationalists' victories after the military collapse of the Ottoman Empire led to the gradual abandonment of its projects for Anatolia. The Arabs, however, who had learned of the Sykes-Picot Agreement through the publication of it, together with other secret treaties of imperial Russia, by the Soviet Russian government late in 1917, were scandalized by it. Their resentment persisted in spite of the modification of its arrangements for the Arab countries by the Allies' Conference of San Remo in April 1920.

Palestine was hard-hit by the war. In addition to the destruction caused by the fighting, the population was devastated by famine, epidemics, and Ottoman punitive measures against Arab nationalists. Major battles took place at Gaza before Jerusalem was captured by British and Allied forces under the command of Gen. Sir Edmund (later 1st Viscount) Allenby in December 1917. The remaining area was occupied by the British by October 1918.

At the war's end, the future of Palestine was problematic. Great Britain, which had set up a military administration in Palestine after capturing Jerusalem, was faced with the problem of having to secure international sanction for the continued occupation of the country in a manner consistent with its ambiguous, seemingly conflicting wartime commitments. On March 20, 1920, delegates from Palestine attended a general Syrian congress at Damascus, which passed a resolution rejecting the Balfour Declaration and elected Fayṣal I — son of Ḥusayn ibn ʿAlī, who ruled the Hejaz — king of a united

Syria (including Palestine). This resolution echoed one passed earlier in Jerusalem, in February 1919, by the first Palestinian Arab conference of Muslim-Christian associations, which had been founded by leading Palestinian Arab notables to oppose Zionist activities. In April 1920, however, at a peace conference held in San Remo, Italy, the Allies divided the former territories of the defeated Ottoman Empire. Of the Ottoman provinces in the Syrian region, the northern portion (Syria and Lebanon) was mandated to France, and the southern portion (Palestine) was mandated to Great Britain. By July 1920 the French had forced Fayṣal to give up his newly founded kingdom of Syria. The hope of founding an Arab Palestine within a federated Syrian state collapsed and with it any prospect of independence. Palestinian Arabs spoke of 1920 as 'ām al-nakbah, the "year of catastrophe."

Uncertainty over the disposition of Palestine affected all its inhabitants and increased political tensions. In April 1920 anti-Zionist riots broke out in the Jewish quarter of Old Jerusalem, killing several and injuring scores. British authorities attributed the riots to Arab disappointment at not having the promises of independence fulfilled and to fears, played on by some Muslim and Christian leaders, of a massive influx of Jews. Following the confirmation of the mandate at San Remo, the British replaced the military administration with a civilian administration in July 1920, and Sir Herbert (later Viscount) Samuel, a Zionist, was appointed the first high commissioner. The new administration proceeded to implement the Balfour Declaration, announcing in August a quota of 16,500 Jewish immigrants for the first year.

In December 1920, Palestinian Arabs at a congress in Haifa established an executive committee (known as the Arab Executive) to act as the representative of the Arabs.

It was never formally recognized by the British and was dissolved in 1934. However, the platform of the Haifa congress, which set out the position that Palestine was an autonomous Arab entity and totally rejected any rights of the Jews to Palestine, remained the basic policy of the Palestinian Arabs until 1948. The arrival of more than 18,000 Jewish immigrants between 1919 and 1921 and land purchases in 1921 by the Jewish National Fund (established in 1901), which led to the eviction of Arab peasants (fellahin), further aroused Arab opposition that was expressed throughout the region through the Christian-Muslim associations.

On May 1, 1921, more serious anti-Zionist riots broke out in Jaffa, spreading to Petaḥ Tiqwa and other Jewish communities, in which nearly 100 were killed. An Arab delegation of notables visited London in August–November 1921, demanding that the Balfour Declaration be repudiated and proposing the creation of a national government with a parliament democratically elected by the country's Muslims, Christians, and Jews. Alarmed by the extent of Arab opposition, the British government issued a White Paper in June 1922 declaring that Great Britain did "not contemplate that Palestine as a whole should be converted into a Jewish National Home, but that such a Home should be founded in Palestine." Immigration would not exceed the economic absorptive capacity of the country, and steps would be taken to set up a legislative council. These proposals were rejected by the Arabs, both because they constituted a large majority of the total mandate population and therefore wished to dominate the instruments of government and rapidly gain independence and because, they argued, the proposals allowed Jewish immigration, which had a political objective, to be regulated by an economic criterion.

THE BRITISH MANDATE

In July 1922 the Council of the League of Nations approved
the mandate instrument for Palestine, including its preamble incorporating the Balfour Declaration and stressing
the Jewish historical connection with Palestine. Article
2 made the mandatory power responsible for placing the
country under such "political, administrative and economic
conditions as will secure the establishment of the Jewish
National Home . . . and the development of self-governing
institutions." Article 4 allowed for the establishment of a
Jewish Agency to advise and cooperate with the Palestine
administration in matters affecting the Jewish national
home. Article 6 required that the Palestine administration,
"while ensuring that the rights and position of other sections of the population are not prejudiced," under suitable
conditions should facilitate Jewish immigration and close
settlement of Jews on the land. Although Transjordan—i.e.,
the lands east of the Jordan River—constituted three-
fourths of the British mandate of Palestine, it was, in spite
of protests from the Zionists, excluded from the clauses
covering the establishment of a Jewish national home. On
Sept. 29, 1923, the mandate officially came into force.

Palestine was a distinct political entity for the first
time in centuries. This created problems and challenges
for Palestinian Arabs and Zionists alike. Both communities realized that by the end of the mandate period the
region's future would be determined by size of population
and ownership of land. Thus the central issues throughout the mandate period were Jewish immigration and land
purchases, with the Jews attempting to increase both and
the Arabs seeking to slow down or halt both. Conflict
over these issues often escalated into violence, and the
British were forced to take action—a lesson not lost on
either side.

Arab nationalist activities became fragmented as tensions arose between clans, religious groups, and city dwellers and fellahin over the issue of how to respond to British rule and the increasing number of Zionists. Moreover, traditional rivalry between the two old preeminent and ambitious Jerusalem families, the Ḥusaynīs and the Nashāshībīs, whose members had held numerous government posts in the late Ottoman period, inhibited the development of effective Arab leadership. Several Arab organizations in the 1920s opposed Jewish immigration, including the Palestine Arab Congress, Muslim-Christian associations, and the Arab Executive. Most Arab groups were led by the strongly anti-British Ḥusaynī family, while the National Defense Party (founded 1934) was under the control of the more accommodating Nashāshībī family. In 1921 the British high commissioner appointed Amīn al-Ḥusaynī to be the (grand) mufti of Jerusalem and made him president of the newly formed Supreme Muslim Council, which controlled the Muslim courts and schools and a considerable portion of the funds raised by religious charitable endowments. Amīn al-Ḥusaynī used this religious position to transform himself into the most powerful political figure among the Arabs.

Initially, the Jews of Palestine thought it best served their interests to cooperate with the British administration. The World Zionist Organization (founded 1897) was regarded as the de facto Jewish Agency stipulated in the mandate, although its president, Chaim Weizmann, remained in London, close to the British government; the Polish-born emigré David Ben-Gurion became the leader of a standing executive in Palestine. Throughout the 1920s most British local authorities in Palestine, especially the military, sympathized with the Palestinian Arabs, whereas the British government in London tended to side with the Zionists. The Jewish community in Palestine, the Yishuv, established its own assembly (Va'ad Leumi), trade union and labour movement (Histadrut), schools, courts, taxation system, medical services, and a number of industrial enterprises. It also formed a military organization called the Haganah. The Jewish Agency came to be controlled by a group called the Labour Zionists, who, for the most part, believed in cooperation with the British and Arabs, but another group, the Revisionist Zionists, founded in 1925 and led by Vladimir Jabotinsky, fully realized that their goal of a Jewish state in all of Palestine (i.e., both sides of the Jordan River) was inconsistent with that of Palestinian Arabs. The Revisionists formed their own military arm, Irgun Zvai Leumi, which did not hesitate to use force against the Arabs.

British rule in Palestine during the mandate was, in general, conscientious, efficient, and responsible. The mandate government developed administrative institutions, municipal services, public works, and transport. It laid water pipelines, expanded ports, extended railway lines, and supplied electricity. It was less assiduous in promoting education, however, particularly in the Arab sector, and it was hampered because it had to respond to outbreaks of violence both between the Arab and Jewish communities and against itself. The aims and aspirations of the three parties in Palestine appeared incompatible, which, as events proved, was indeed the case.

There was little political cooperation between Arabs and Jews in Palestine. In 1923 the British high commissioner tried to win Arab cooperation by offers first of a legislative council that would reflect the Arab majority and then of an Arab agency. Both offers were rejected by the Arabs as falling far short of their national demands. Nor did the Arabs wish to legitimize a situation they rejected in principle. The years 1923–29 were relatively quiet; Arab passivity was partly due to the drop in Jewish immigration in 1926–28. In 1927 the number of Jewish emigrants exceeded that of immigrants, and in 1928 there was a net Jewish immigration of only 10 persons.

Nevertheless, the Jewish national home continued to consolidate itself in terms of urban, agricultural, social, cultural, and industrial development. Large amounts of land were purchased from Arab owners, who often were absentee landlords. In August 1929 negotiations were concluded for the formation of an enlarged Jewish Agency to include non-Zionist Jewish sympathizers throughout the world.

This last development, while accentuating Arab fears, gave the Zionists a new sense of confidence. In the same month, a dispute in Jerusalem concerning religious practices at the Western Wall—sacred to Jews as the only remnant of the Second Temple of Jerusalem and to Muslims as the site of the Dome of the Rock—flared up into serious communal clashes in Jerusalem, Zefat, and Hebron. Some 250 were killed and 570 wounded, the Arab casualties being mostly at the hands of British security forces. A royal commission of inquiry under the aegis of Sir Walter Shaw attributed the clashes to the fact that "the Arabs have come to see in Jewish immigration not only a menace to their livelihood but a possible overlord of the future." A second royal commission, headed by Sir John Hope Simpson, issued a report stating that there was at that time no margin of land available for agricultural settlement by new immigrants. These two reports raised in an acute form the question of where Britain's duty lay if its specific obligations to the Zionists under the Balfour Declaration clashed with its general obligations to the Arabs under Article 22 of the Covenant of the League of Nations. They also formed the basis of the Passfield White Paper, issued in October 1930, which accorded some priority to Britain's obligations to the Arabs. Not only did it call for a halt to Jewish immigration, but it also recommended that land be sold only to landless Arabs and that the determination of "economic absorptive capacity" be based on levels of Arab as well as Jewish unemployment. This was seen by the Zionists as cutting at the root of their program, for, if the right of the Arab resident were to gain priority over that of the Jewish immigrant, whether actual or potential, development of the Jewish national home would come to a standstill.

In response to protests from Palestinian Jews and London Zionists, the British prime minister, Ramsay MacDonald, in February 1931 addressed an explanatory letter to Chaim Weizmann nullifying the Passfield White Paper, which virtually meant a return to the policy of the 1922 White Paper. This letter convinced the Arabs that recommendations in their favour made in Palestine could be annulled by Zionist influence at the centre of power in London. In December 1931 a Muslim congress at Jerusalem was attended by delegates from 22 countries to warn against the danger of Zionism.

From the early 1930s onward, developments in Europe once again began to impose themselves more forcefully on Palestine. The Nazi accession to power in Germany in 1933 and the widespread persecution of Jews throughout central and eastern Europe gave a great impetus to Jewish immigration, which jumped to 30,000 in 1933, 42,000 in 1934, and 61,000 in 1935. By 1936 the Jewish population of Palestine had reached almost 400,000, or one-third of the total. This new wave of immigration provoked major acts of violence against Jews and the British in 1933 and 1935. The Arab population of Palestine also grew rapidly, largely by natural increase, although some Arabs were attracted from outside the region by the capital infusion brought by middle-class Jewish immigrants and British public works. Most of the Arabs (nearly nine-tenths) continued to be employed in agriculture in spite of deteriorating economic conditions. By the mid-1930s, however, many landless Arabs had joined the expanding Arab proletariat working in the construction trades on the edge of rapidly growing urban centres. This was the beginning of a shift in the foundations of Palestinian economic and social life that was to have profound immediate and long-term effects.

In November 1935 the Arab political parties collectively demanded that Jewish immigration cease, land transfer be prohibited, and democratic institutions be established. A boycott of Zionist and British goods was proclaimed. In December the British administration offered to set up a legislative council of 28 members, in which the Arabs (both Muslim and Christian) would have a majority. The British would retain control through their selection of nonelected members. Although Arabs would not be represented in the council in proportion to their numbers, Arab leaders favoured the proposal, but the Zionists criticized it bitterly as an attempt to freeze the national home through a constitutional Arab stranglehold. In any event, London rejected the proposal. This, together with the example of rising nationalism in neighbouring Egypt and Syria, increasing unemployment in Palestine, and a poor citrus harvest, touched off a long-smoldering Arab rebellion.

THE ARAB REVOLT

The Arab Revolt of 1936–39 was the first sustained violent uprising of Palestinian Arabs in more than a century. Thousands of Arabs from all classes were mobilized, and nationalistic sentiment was fanned in the Arabic press, schools, and literary circles. The British, taken aback by the extent and intensity of the revolt, shipped more than 20,000 troops into Palestine, and by 1939 the Zionists had armed more than 15,000 Jews in their own nationalist movement.

The revolt began with spontaneous acts of violence committed by the religiously and nationalistically

motivated followers of Sheikh 'Izz al-Dīn al-Qassām, who
had been killed by the British in 1935. In April 1936 the murder of two Jews led to escalating violence, and Qassāmite
groups initiated a general strike in Jaffa and Nāblus. At that
point the Arab political parties formed an Arab Higher
Committee presided over by the mufti of Jerusalem, Amīn
al-Husaynī. It called for a general strike, nonpayment of
taxes, and the closing of municipal governments (although
government employees were allowed to stay at work) and
demanded an end to Jewish immigration, a ban on land
sales to Jews, and national independence.

Simultaneously with the strike, Arab rebels, joined
by volunteers from neighbouring Arab countries, took to
the hills, attacking Jewish settlements and British installations in the northern part of the country. By the end of
the year, the movement had assumed the dimensions of a
national revolt, the mainstay of which was the Arab peas-
antry. Even though the arrival of British troops restored

*A group of men display their firepower in 1938, a period of Arab revolt. Arab
forces gathered in the hills of northern Palestine, staging attacks on Jewish
settlements and British forces.* Popperfoto/Getty Images

some semblance of order, the armed rebellion, arson, bombings, and assassinations continued.

A royal commission of inquiry presided over by Lord Robert Peel, which was sent to investigate the volatile situation, reported in July 1937 that the revolt was caused by Arab desire for independence and fear of the Jewish national home. The Peel Commission declared the mandate unworkable and Britain's obligations to Arabs and Jews mutually irreconcilable. In the face of what it described as "right against right," the commission recommended that the region be partitioned.

Peel Commission

The Peel Commission (known in full as the Royal Commission of Inquiry to Palestine) was a group headed by Lord Robert Peel that was appointed in 1936 by the British government to investigate the causes of unrest among Palestinian Arabs and Jews.

Discontent in Palestine intensified after 1920, when the Conference of San Remo awarded the British government a mandate to control Palestine. With its formal approval by the League of Nations in 1922, this mandate incorporated the Balfour Declaration of 1917, which provided for both the establishment of a Jewish national home in Palestine and the preservation of the civil and religious (but not the political or national) rights of non-Jewish Palestinian communities. Palestinian Arabs, desiring political autonomy and resenting the continued Jewish immigration into Palestine, disapproved of the mandate, and by 1936 their dissatisfaction had grown into open rebellion.

The Peel Commission published its report in July 1937. The report admitted that the mandate was unworkable because Jewish and Arab objectives in Palestine were incompatible, and it proposed that Palestine be partitioned into three zones: an Arab state, a Jewish state, and a neutral territory containing the holy places. Although the British government initially accepted these proposals, by 1938 it had recognized that such partitioning would be infeasible, and it ultimately rejected the commission's report.

The Zionist attitude toward partition, though ambiva-
lent, was overall one of cautious acceptance. For the first
time a British official body explicitly spoke of a Jewish state.
The commission not only allotted to this state an area that
was immensely larger than the existing Jewish landholdings
but recommended the forcible transfer of the Arab population from the proposed Jewish state. The Zionists, however,
still needed mandatory protection for their further development and left the door open for an undivided Palestine.
The Arabs were horrified by the idea of dismembering the
region and particularly by the suggestion that they be forcibly transferred (to Transjordan). As a result, the momentum
of the revolt increased during 1937 and 1938.

In September 1937 the British were forced to declare
martial law. The Arab Higher Committee was dissolved,
and many officials of the Supreme Muslim Council and
other organizations were arrested. The mufti fled to
Lebanon and then Iraq, never to return to an undivided
Palestine. Although the Arab Revolt continued well into
1939, high casualty rates and firm British measures gradually eroded its strength. According to some estimates,
more than 5,000 Arabs were killed, 15,000 wounded, and
5,600 imprisoned during the revolt. Although it signified
the birth of a national identity, the revolt was unsuccessful
in many ways. The general strike, which was called off in
October 1939, had encouraged Zionist self-reliance, and
the Arabs of Palestine were unable to recover from their
sustained effort of defying the British administration.
Their traditional leaders were either killed, arrested, or
deported, leaving the dispirited and disarmed population
divided along urban-rural, class, clan, and religious lines.
The Zionists, on the other hand, were united behind Ben-
Gurion, and the Haganah had been given permission to
arm itself. It cooperated with British forces and the Irgun
Zvai Leumi in attacks against Arabs.

However, the prospect of war in Europe alarmed the British government and caused it to reassess its policy in Palestine. If Britain went to war, it could not afford to face Arab hostility in Palestine and in neighbouring countries. The Woodhead Commission, under Sir John Woodhead, was set up to examine the practicality of partition. In November 1938 it recommended against the Peel Commission's plan—largely on the ground that the number of Arabs in the proposed Jewish state would be almost equal to the number of Jews—and put forward alternative proposals drastically reducing the area of the Jewish state and limiting the sovereignty of the proposed states. This was unacceptable to both Arabs and Jews. Seeking to find a solution acceptable to both parties, the British announced the impracticability of partition and called for a roundtable conference in London.

No agreement was reached at the London conference held during February and March 1939. In May 1939, however, the British government issued a White Paper, which essentially yielded to Arab demands. It stated that the Jewish national home should be established within an independent Palestinian state. During the next five years 75,000 Jews would be allowed into the country; thereafter Jewish immigration would be subject to Arab "acquiescence." Land transfer to Jews would be allowed only in certain areas in Palestine, and an independent Palestinian state would be considered within 10 years. The Arabs, although in favour of the new policy, rejected the White Paper, largely because they mistrusted the British government and opposed a provision contained in the paper for extending the mandate beyond the 10-year period. The Zionists were shocked and enraged by the paper, which they considered a death blow to their program and to Jews who desperately sought refuge in Palestine from the growing persecution they were enduring in Europe. The

1939 White Paper marked the end of the Anglo-Zionist entente.

Progress toward a Jewish national home had, however, been remarkable since 1918. Although the majority of the Jewish population was urban, the number of rural Zionist colonies had increased from 47 to about 200. Between 1922 and 1940 Jewish landholdings had risen from about 148,500 to 383,500 acres (about 60,100 to 155,200 hectares) and now constituted roughly one-seventh of the cultivatable land, and the Jewish population had grown from 83,790 to some 467,000, or nearly one-third of a total population of about 1,528,000. Tel Aviv had developed into an all-Jewish city of 150,000 inhabitants, and hundreds of millions of dollars of Jewish capital had been introduced into the region. The Jewish literacy rate was high, schools were expanding, and the Hebrew language had become widespread. In spite of a split in 1935 between the mainline Zionists and the radical Revisionists, who advocated the use of force to establish the Zionist state, Zionist institutions in Palestine became stronger in the 1930s and helped create the preconditions for the establishment of a Jewish state.

WORLD WAR II

With the outbreak of World War II in September 1939, Zionist and British policies came into direct conflict. Throughout the war Zionists sought with growing urgency to increase Jewish immigration to Palestine, while the British sought to prevent such immigration, regarding it as illegal and a threat to the stability of a region essential to the war effort. Ben-Gurion declared on behalf of the Jewish Agency, "We shall fight [beside Great Britain in] this war as if there was no White Paper and we shall fight the White Paper as if there was no war." British attempts to prevent Jewish immigration to Palestine in the face of the Holocaust—the terrible tragedy befalling European Jewry and others deemed undesirable by the Nazis—led to the disastrous sinking of two ships carrying Jewish refugees, the *Patria* (November 1940) and the *Struma* (February 1942). In response, the Irgun, under the leadership of Menachem Begin, and a small militant splinter group, Lehi (Fighters for the Freedom of Israel), known for its founder as the Stern Gang, embarked on widespread attacks on the British, culminating in the murder of Lord Moyne, British minister of state, by two Lehi members in Cairo in November 1944.

During the war years the Jewish community in Palestine was vastly strengthened. Its moderate wing supported the British; in September 1944 a Jewish brigade was formed—a total of 27,000 Jews having enlisted in the British forces—and attached to the British 8th Army. Jewish industry in general was given immense impetus by the war, and a Jewish munitions industry developed to manufacture antitank mines for the British forces. For the Yishuv the war and the Holocaust confirmed that a Jewish state must be established in Palestine. Important also was the support of American Zionists. In May 1942, at a Zionist conference held at the Biltmore Hotel in New York City, Ben-Gurion gained support for a program demanding unrestricted immigration, a Jewish army, and the establishment of Palestine as a Jewish commonwealth.

The Arabs of Palestine remained largely quiescent throughout the war. Amīn al-Ḥusaynī had fled—by way of Iraq, Iran, Turkey, and Italy—to Germany, whence he broadcast appeals to his fellow Arabs to ally with the Axis powers against Britain and Zionism. Yet the mufti failed to rally Palestinian Arabs to the Axis cause. Although some supported Germany, the majority supported the Allies, and approximately 23,000 Arabs enlisted in the British forces (especially in the Arab Legion). Increases in agricultural prices benefited the Arab peasants, who began to pay accumulated debts. However, the Arab Revolt had ruined many Arab merchants and importers, and British war activities, although bringing new levels of prosperity, further weakened the traditional social institutions—the family and village—by fostering a large urban Arab working class.

The Allied discovery of the Nazi extermination camps at the end of World War II and the undecided future of Holocaust survivors led to an increasing number of pro-Zionist statements from U.S. politicians. In August 1945 U.S. Pres. Harry S. Truman requested that British Prime Minister Clement Attlee facilitate the immediate admission of 100,000 Jewish Holocaust survivors into Palestine, and in December the U.S. Senate and House of Representatives asked for unrestricted Jewish immigration to the limit of the economic absorptive capacity of Palestine. Truman's request signaled the U.S. entry into the arena of powers determining the future of Palestine. The question of Palestine, now linked with the fate of Holocaust survivors, became once again the focus of international attention.

As the war came to an end, the neighbouring Arab countries began to take a more direct interest in Palestine. In October 1944 Arab heads of state met in Alexandria, Egypt, and issued a statement, the Alexandria Protocol, setting out the Arab position. They made clear that, although they regretted the bitter fate inflicted upon European Jewry by European dictatorships, the issue of European Jewish survivors ought not to be confused with Zionism. Solving the problem of European Jewry, they asserted, should not be achieved by inflicting injustice on Palestinian Arabs. The covenant of the League of Arab States, or Arab League, formed in March 1945, contained an annex emphasizing the Arab character of Palestine. The Arab League appointed an Arab Higher Executive for Palestine (the Arab Higher Committee), which included a broad spectrum of Palestinian leaders, to speak for the Palestinian Arabs. In December 1945 the league declared a boycott of Zionist goods. The pattern of the postwar struggle for Palestine was unmistakably emerging.

The Early Postwar Period

The major issue between 1945 and 1948 was, as it had been throughout the mandate, Jewish immigration to Palestine. The Yishuv was determined to remove all restrictions to Jewish immigration and to establish a Jewish state. The Arabs were determined that no more Jews should arrive and that Palestine should achieve independence as an Arab state. The primary goal of British policy following World War II was to secure British strategic interests in the Middle East and Asia. Because the cooperation of the Arab states was considered essential to this goal, British Foreign Secretary Ernest Bevin opposed Jewish immigration and the foundation of an independent Jewish state in Palestine. The U.S. State Department basically supported the British position, but Truman was determined to ensure that Jews displaced by the war were permitted to enter Palestine. The issue was resolved in 1948 when the British mandate collapsed under the pressure of force and diplomacy.

In November 1945, in an effort to secure American coresponsibility for a Palestinian policy, Bevin announced the formation of an Anglo-American Committee of Inquiry. Pending the report of the committee, Jewish immigration would continue at the rate of 1,500 persons per month above the 75,000 limit set by the 1939 White Paper. A plan of provincial autonomy for Arabs and Jews was worked out in an Anglo-American conference in 1946 and became the basis for discussions in London between Great Britain and the representatives of Arabs and Zionists.

In the meantime, Zionist pressure in Palestine was intensified by the unauthorized immigration of refugees on a hitherto unprecedented scale and by closely coordinated attacks by Zionist underground forces. Jewish immigration was impelled by the burning memories of the Holocaust, the chaotic postwar conditions in Europe, and the growing possibility of attaining a Jewish state where the victims of persecution could guarantee their own safety. The underground's attacks culminated in Jerusalem on July 22, 1946, when the Irgun blew up a part of the King David Hotel containing British government and military offices, with the loss of 91 lives.

On the Arab side, a meeting of the Arab states took place in June 1946 at Blūdān, Syria, at which secret resolutions were adopted threatening British and American interests in the Middle East if Arab rights were disregarded. In Palestine the Ḥusaynīs consolidated their power, in spite of widespread mistrust of the mufti, who now resided in Egypt.

While Zionists pressed ahead with immigration and attacks on the government, and Arab states mobilized in response, British resolve to remain in the Middle East was collapsing. World War II had left Britain victorious but exhausted. After the war it lacked the funds and political will to maintain control of colonial possessions that were agitating, with increasing violence, for independence. When a conference called in London in February 1947 failed to resolve the impasse, Great Britain, already negotiating its withdrawal from India and eager to decrease its costly military presence in Palestine (of the more than 280,000 troops stationed there during the war, more than 80,000 still remained), referred the Palestine question to the United Nations (UN). On August 31 a majority report of the UN Special Committee on Palestine (UNSCOP) recommended that the region be partitioned into an Arab and a Jewish state, which, however, should retain an economic union. Jerusalem and its environs were to be international. These recommendations were substantially adopted by a two-thirds majority of the UN General Assembly in Resolution 181, dated Nov. 29, 1947, a decision made possible partly because of an agreement between the United States and the Soviet Union on partition and partly because pressure was exerted on some small countries by Zionist sympathizers in the United States. All the Islamic Asian countries voted against partition, and an Arab proposal to query the International Court of Justice on the competence of the General Assembly to partition a country against the wishes of the majority of its inhabitants (in 1946 there were 1,269,000 Arabs and 678,000 Jews in Palestine) was narrowly defeated.

The Zionists welcomed the partition proposal both because it recognized a Jewish state and because it allotted slightly more than half of (west-of-Jordan) Palestine to it. As in 1937, the Arabs fiercely opposed partition both in principle and because nearly half of the population of the Jewish state would be Arab. Resolution 181 called for the formation of the UN Palestine Commission—which it tasked with selecting and overseeing provisional councils of government for the Jewish and Arab states by April 1, 1948—and set the date for the termination of the mandate no later than Aug. 1, 1948. The British later announced that the mandate would be terminated on May 15, 1948.

CIVIL WAR IN PALESTINE

Soon after the UN resolution, fighting broke out in Palestine. The Zionists mobilized their forces and redoubled their efforts to bring in immigrants. In December 1947 the Arab League pledged its support to the Palestinian Arabs and organized a force of 3,000 volunteers. Civil war spread, and external intervention increased as the disintegration of the British administration progressed.

Alarmed by the continued fighting, the United States in early March 1948 expressed its opposition to forcibly implementing a partition. A March 12 report by the UN Palestine Commission stated that the establishment of provisional councils of government able to fulfill their functions would be impossible by April 1. Arab resistance to the partition in principle precluded the establishment of an Arab council, and, although steps had been taken toward the selection of the Jewish council, the commission reported that the latter council would be unable to carry out its functions as intended by the resolution. Hampering efforts altogether was Great Britain's refusal in any case to share with the commission the administration of Palestine during the transitional period. On March 19 the United States called for the UN Palestine Commission to suspend its efforts. On March 30 the United States proposed that a truce be declared and that the problem be further considered by the General Assembly.

The Zionists, insisting that partition was binding and anxious about the change in U.S. policy, made a major effort to establish their state. They launched two offensives during April. The success of these operations coincided roughly with the failure of an Arab attack on the Zionist settlement of Mishmar Ha 'Emeq; the death in battle of an Arab national hero, 'Abd al-Qādir al-Husaynī, in command of the Jerusalem front; and the massacre, by Irgunists and members of the Stern Gang, of civilian inhabitants of the Arab village of Dayr Yāsīn. On April 22 Haifa fell to the Zionists, and Jaffa, after severe mortar shelling, surrendered to them on May 13. Simultaneously with their military offensives, the Zionists launched a campaign of psychological warfare. The Arabs of Palestine, divided, badly led, and reliant on the regular armies of the Arab states, became demoralized, and their efforts to prevent partition collapsed.

On May 14 the last British high commissioner, Gen. Sir Alan Cunningham, left Palestine. On the same day the State of Israel was declared and within a few hours won de facto recognition from the United States and de jure recognition from the Soviet Union. Early on May 15 units of the regular armies of Syria, Lebanon, Transjordan, Iraq, and Egypt crossed the frontiers of Palestine.

In a series of campaigns alternating with truces between May and December 1948, the Arab units were routed, and by the summer of 1949 Israel had concluded armistices with its neighbours. It had also been recognized by more than 50 governments throughout the world, joined the UN, and established its sovereignty over about 8,000 square miles (21,000 square km) of formerly mandated Palestine west of the Jordan River. The remaining 2,000 square miles (5,200 square km) were divided between Transjordan and Egypt. Transjordan retained the lands on the west bank of the Jordan River, including the eastern portion of Jerusalem (East Jerusalem), although its annexation of those lands in 1950 was not generally recognized as legitimate. In 1949 the name of the expanded country was changed to the Hashimite Kingdom of Jordan. Egypt retained control of, but did not annex, a small area on the Mediterranean coast that became known as the Gaza Strip. The Palestinian Arab community ceased to exist as a cohesive social and political entity.

CHAPTER 2

TOWARD THE EMERGENCE OF PALESTINIAN AUTONOMY

With the partition of Palestine and the establishment of the State of Israel in 1948, the status of the Palestinian community, including the refugees generated by the conflict, was cast into uncertainty. The move toward Palestinian autonomy in subsequent decades remained a central aim, although how it was to be achieved was not always clear.

THE PARTITION OF PALESTINE AND ITS AFTERMATH (1948–67)

If one chief theme in the post-1948 pattern was embattled Israel and a second the hostility of its Arab neighbours, a third was the plight of the huge number of Arab refugees. The violent birth of Israel led to a major displacement of the Arab population, who either were driven out by Zionist military forces before May 15, 1948, by the Israeli army after that date, or fled for fear of violence by these forces. Many wealthy merchants and leading urban notables from Jaffa, Tel Aviv, Haifa, and Jerusalem fled to Lebanon, Egypt, and Jordan, while the middle class tended to move to all-Arab towns such as Nāblus and Nazareth. The majority of fellahin ended up in refugee camps. More than 400 Arab villages disappeared, and Arab life in the coastal cities (especially Jaffa and Haifa) virtually disintegrated. The centre of Palestinian life shifted to the Arab towns of the hilly eastern portion of the region—which was immediately west of the Jordan River and came to be called the West Bank.

Like everything else in the Arab-Israeli conflict, population figures are hotly disputed. Nearly 1.4 million Arabs lived in Palestine when the war broke out.

Arab refugees displaced by the conflict in Palestine await transport on a British ship in 1948. John Phillips/Time & Life Pictures/Getty Images

Estimates of the number of Arabs displaced from their original homes, villages, and neighbourhoods during the period from December 1947 to January 1949 range from about 520,000 to about one million. There is general consensus, however, that the actual number was more than 600,000 and likely exceeded 700,000. Some 276,000 moved to the West Bank; by 1949 more than half the prewar Arab population of Palestine lived in the West Bank (from 400,000 in 1947 to more than 700,000). Between 160,000 and 190,000 fled to the Gaza Strip. More than one-fifth of Palestinian Arabs left Palestine altogether. About 100,000 of these went to Lebanon, 100,000 to Jordan, between 75,000 and 90,000 to Syria, 7,000 to 10,000 to Egypt, and 4,000 to Iraq.

THE TERM "PALESTINIAN"

Henceforth the term "Palestinian" will be used when referring to the Arabs of the former mandated Palestine, excluding Israel. Although the Arabs of Palestine had been creating and developing a Palestinian identity for about 200 years, the idea that Palestinians form a distinct people is relatively recent. The Arabs living in Palestine had never had a separate state. Until the establishment of Israel, the term "Palestinian" was used by Jews and foreigners to describe the inhabitants of Palestine and had only begun to be used by the Arabs themselves at the turn of the 20th century. At the same time, most saw themselves as part of the larger Arab or Muslim community. The Arabs of Palestine began widely using the term "Palestinian" starting in the pre-World War I period to indicate the nationalist concept of a Palestinian people. But after 1948 — and even more so after 1967 — for Palestinians themselves the term came to signify not only a place of origin but, more importantly, a sense of a shared past and future in the form of a Palestinian state.

THE ISRAELI ARABS

Approximately 150,000 Arabs remained in Israel when the Israeli state was founded. These Israeli Arabs represented about one-eighth of all Palestinians and by 1952 roughly the same proportion of the Israeli population. The majority of them lived in villages in western Galilee. Because much of their land was confiscated, Arabs were forced to abandon agriculture and become unskilled wage labourers, working in Jewish industries and construction companies. As citizens of the State of Israel, in theory they were guaranteed equal religious and civil rights with Jews. In reality, however, until 1966 they lived under a military jurisdiction that imposed severe restrictions on their political options and freedom of movement. Most of them remained politically quiescent, and many accepted Zionist Israel as a reality and sought to ameliorate their circumstances through electoral participation, education, and economic integration.

Israel sought to impede the development of a cohesive national consciousness among the Palestinians by dealing with various minority groups, such as Druze, Circassians, and Bedouin; hindering the work of the Muslim religious organizations; arresting and harassing individuals suspected of harbouring nationalist sentiments; and focusing on education as a means of creating a new Israeli Arab identity. By the late 1960s, as agriculture declined and social customs related to such events as bride selection and marriage broke down, the old patriarchal clan system had all but collapsed. For almost 20 years after Israel was established, Israeli Arabs were isolated from other Arabs.

WEST BANK (AND JORDANIAN) PALESTINIANS

The Jordanian monarchy saw in the events of 1948–49 the opportunity to expand Jordanian territory and integrate Palestinians into its population, thereby creating a new Jordanian nationality. Through a series of political and social policies, Jordan sought to consolidate its control over the political future of Palestinians and to become their speaker. It provided education and, in 1949, extended citizenship to Palestinians. A majority of all Palestinians became Jordanian citizens. However, tensions soon developed between original Jordanian citizens and the better-educated, more skilled newcomers. Wealthy Palestinians lived in the towns of the eastern and western sides of the Jordan River, competing for positions within the government, while the fellahin filled the UN refugee camps.

Palestinians constituted about two-thirds of the population of Jordan. Half the seats in the Jordanian Chamber of Deputies were reserved for representatives from the West Bank, but this measure and similar attempts to integrate the West Bank with the area lying east of the Jordan River were made difficult by the significant social, economic, educational, and political differences between the residents of each. Jordanian Palestinians, other than the notable families favoured by the Jordanian monarchy, tended to support the radical pan-Arab and anti-Israeli policies of Egypt's Pres. Gamal Abdel Nasser rather than the more cautious and conciliatory position of Jordan's King Hussein.

PALESTINIANS IN THE GAZA STRIP

During the 20 years the Gaza Strip was under Egyptian control (1948–67), it remained little more than a reservation.

Egyptian rule was generally repressive. Palestinians living in the region were denied citizenship, which rendered them stateless (i.e., it left them without citizenship of any country), and they were allowed little real control over local administration. They were, however, allowed to attend Egyptian universities and, at times, to elect local officials.

In 1948 Amīn al-Ḥusaynī declared a Government of All Palestine in the Gaza Strip. However, because it was totally dependent on Egypt, it was short-lived. The failure of this venture and al-Ḥusaynī's lack of credibility because of his collaboration with the Axis powers during World War II did much to weaken Palestinian Arab nationalism in the 1950s.

The Gaza Strip, 25 miles (40 km) long and 4–5 miles (6–8 km) wide, became one of the most densely populated areas of the world, with more than four-fifths of its population urban. Poverty and social misery became characteristic of life in the region. The rate of unemployment was high; many of the Palestinians lived in refugee camps, depending primarily on UN aid. Most of the agricultural lands they had formerly worked were now inaccessible, and little or no industry was allowed, but commerce flourished as Gaza became a kind of duty-free port for Egyptians. Although some Gaza Strip Palestinians were able to leave the territory and gain an education and find employment elsewhere, most had no alternative but to stay in the area, in spite of its lack of natural resources and jobs.

UNRWA CAMPS

In December 1949 the UN General Assembly created the United Nations Relief and Works Agency for Palestine Refugees in the Near East (UNRWA) to assist the Palestinian refugees. In May 1950 UNRWA established a total of 53 refugee "camps" on both sides of the Jordan

River and in the Gaza Strip, Lebanon, and Syria to assist the hundreds of thousands of Arab refugees it calculated needed help. Initially refugees in the improvised camps lived in tents, but after 1958 these were replaced by small houses of concrete blocks with iron roofs. Conditions were extremely harsh; often several families had to share one tent, and exposure to the extreme winter and summer temperatures inflicted additional suffering. Loss of home and income lowered morale. Although the refugees were provided with rent-free accommodations and basic services such as water, health care, and education (UNRWA ran both elementary and secondary schools in the camps, teaching more than 40,000 students by 1951), poverty and misery were widespread. Work was scarce, even though UNRWA sought to integrate the Palestinians into the depressed economies of the "host" countries.

Palestinians who continued to live in refugee camps felt a greater sense of alienation and dislocation than the more fortunate ones who found jobs and housing and became integrated into the national economies of the countries in which they resided. Although the camps strengthened family and village ties, their demoralized inhabitants were isolated from mainstream Palestinian political activities during the 1950s.

PALESTINIANS OUTSIDE MANDATED PALESTINE

Palestinians found employment in Syria, Iraq, Lebanon, and the Persian Gulf states, but only a few were able to become citizens of those countries. Often they were the victims of discrimination, as well as being closely supervised by the respective governments intent on limiting their political activities.

United Nations Relief and Works Agency for Palestine Refugees in the Near East (UNRWA)

UNRWA is a subsidiary agency created by the United Nations (UN) General Assembly in 1949 to provide relief, health, and education services for Palestinians who lost both their homes and means of livelihood during the Arab-Israeli wars following the establishment of the state of Israel in 1948. UNRWA began operations in 1950 and was originally headquartered in Beirut, although it was moved to Vienna in 1978. In 1996 the General Assembly moved the agency to the Gaza Strip to demonstrate the Assembly's commitment to the Arab-Israeli peace process.

Hundreds of thousands of Palestinians originally qualified for relief, and by the late 20th century there were nearly four million registered Palestinian refugees, including the children of the original refugees. As the largest UN operation in the Middle East and one of the biggest employers in the region—with service operations in Jordan, Lebanon, Syria, the West Bank, and the Gaza Strip—UNRWA provides camps, food, clothing, schools, vocational training, and health clinics, often working in cooperation with the World Health Organization (WHO), the United Nations Children's Fund (UNICEF), the United Nations Population Fund (UNFPA), and the United Nations Educational, Scientific and Cultural Organization (UNESCO).

UNRWA is financed by voluntary contributions of UN member states. Like its predecessor organization, the UN Relief for Palestine Refugees in the Near East, it was originally designed as a temporary agency, though its mandate has been continuously renewed by the General Assembly. Its chief officer, the commissioner-general—the only leader of a UN agency to report directly to the General Assembly—is appointed by the UN secretary-general with the approval of an Advisory Commission.

RESURGENCE OF
PALESTINIAN IDENTITY

The events of 1948 (also called by Palestinians *al-nakbah*, "the catastrophe") and the experience of exile shaped Palestinian political and cultural activity for the next generation. The central task of reconstruction fell to Palestinians living outside Israel—both in the West Bank and Gaza communities and in the new Palestinian communities outside the former British mandate. (Arabs living within the State of Israel remained in an ambiguous, isolated situation and were regarded with some suspicion by both Israelis and Palestinians.) The new leaders came disproportionately from among those who had moved to various Middle Eastern states and to the West, even though four out of five Palestinians had remained within the borders of the former British mandate. By the mid-1960s, in spite of Israeli efforts to forestall the emergence of a new Palestinian identity, a young, educated leadership had arisen, replacing the discredited traditional local and clan leaders.

THE ROLE OF CAMPS

Palestinian refugee camps differed depending on the country in which they were located, but they shared one common development—the emergence of a "diaspora consciousness." In time this consciousness grew into a renewed national identity and reinvigorated social institutions, leading to the establishment of more complex social and political structures by the 1960s. A new Palestinian leadership emerged from the schools UNRWA had established, as well as from the universities of Egypt, Syria, Lebanon, western Europe, and the United States. Palestinians living in UNRWA-administered refugee camps felt isolated, politically powerless, disoriented, bit-ter, and resentful. They remained unassimilated and were generating a new sense of identity based on a pan-Arabism inspired by Nasser, the cultivated memory of a lost para-dise (Palestine), and an emerging pan-Islamic movement.

The Role of Palestinians Outside Formerly Mandated Palestine

By the late 1960s a class of educated and mobile Palestinians had emerged, with fewer than half of them living in the West Bank or Gaza. They were working in the oil com-panies, civil services, and educational institutions of most Arab states in the Middle East. Having successfully resisted the efforts of Amīn al-Ḥusaynī, Jordan, and Egypt to control and speak for them, they joined the process of reshaping Palestinian consciousness and institutions. Thus Palestinians entered a new stage of the struggle for nationhood.

The Palestine Liberation Organization

An Arab summit meeting in Cairo in 1964 led to the for-mation of the Palestine Liberation Organization (PLO). A political umbrella organization of several Palestinian groups, the PLO thereafter consistently claimed to be the sole representative of all Palestinian people. Its first leader was Aḥmad Shuqayrī, a protégé of Egypt. In its charter (the Palestine National Charter, or Covenant) the PLO delineated its basic principles and goals, the most important of which were the right to an independent state, the total liberation of Palestine, and the destruction of the State of Israel.

A Palestine National Council (PNC) was established to serve as the supreme body, or parliament, of the PLO,

Aḥmad Shuqayrī, the first leader of the Palestinian Liberation Organization (PLO). The PLO unified various groups that sought an autonomous Palestinian state. Keystone/Hulton Archive/Getty Images

and an executive committee was formed to manage PLO activities. Initially, the PNC consisted of civilian representatives from various areas, including Jordan, the West Bank, and the Persian Gulf states, but representatives of guerrilla organizations were added in 1968.

FATAH AND OTHER GUERRILLA ORGANIZATIONS

Several years before the creation of the PLO, a secret organization had been formed: the Palestine National Liberation Movement (Ḥarakat al-Taḥrīr al-Waṭanī al-Filasṭīnī), known from a reversal of its Arabic initials as Fatah. Both the PLO and Fatah undertook the training of guerrilla units for raids on Israel. In addition to Fatah, the largest and most influential guerrilla organization, several others emerged in the late 1960s. The most important ones were the Popular Front for the Liberation of Palestine (PFLP), the Democratic Front for the Liberation of Palestine (DFLP), the Popular Front for the Liberation of Palestine–General Command (PFLP–GC, a splinter group from the PFLP), and al-Ṣā'iqah (backed by Syria). These groups joined forces inside the PLO in spite of their differences in ideology and tactics (some were dedicated to openly terrorist tactics). In 1969 Yāsir 'Arafāt, leader of Fatah, became chairman of the PLO's executive committee and thus the chief of the Palestinian national movement.

Popular Front for the Liberation of Palestine (PFLP)

The PFLP (Arabic: al-Jabhah al-Sha'biyyah li-Taḥrīr Filasṭīn) is an organization providing an institutional framework for militant organizations associated with the PLO, notable for its Marxist-Leninist ideology and its hijacking of a number of aircraft between 1968 and 1974.

The PFLP was established in 1967 in an amalgamation of three different guerrilla groups by the militant Palestinian leader George Ḥabash. Conflicts within the organization over ideology led to several splits and generated independent factions, most notably the PFLP-General Command (PFLP-GC) established in 1968 by Aḥmad Jibrīl. Each of these factions engaged in guerrilla activity against Israel and often undertook acts of terrorism against the Jewish state and Western interests. The PFLP itself carried out or organized many notorious attacks against Israeli and Western targets, most notably the hijacking and destruction of several commercial airliners in the late 1960s and early '70s. The PFLP rejected political compromise with Israel—it opposed the peace process begun with Israel in the 1990s—and pledged to replace that state with a secular, democratic state in Palestine. It took a vigorously anti-Western and anticapitalist stance on other Middle Eastern questions. Ḥabash retired as head of the organization in 2000; his successor, Abū 'Alī Muṣṭafā, was killed by Israeli forces in the PFLP's West Bank offices in 2001.

In spite of their differences in tactics and ideology, the guerrilla organizations were united in rejecting any political settlement that did not include what they characterized as the total liberation of Palestine and the return of the refugees to their homeland, goals that were to be achieved through armed struggle. Palestinian spokesmen claimed, however, that, while they aimed at dismantling Israel and purging Palestine of Zionism, they also sought to establish a nonsectarian state in which Jews, Christians, and Muslims could live in equality. Most Israelis doubted the sincerity or practicality of this goal and viewed the PLO as a terrorist organization committed to destroying not only the Zionist state but Israeli Jews.

THE ARAB-ISRAELI WAR OF 1967 AND ITS CONSEQUENCES

In the June (Six-Day) War of 1967, Israel defeated the combined forces of Egypt, Syria, and Jordan and also overran large tracts of territory, including East Jerusalem, the West Bank (known to Israelis by the biblical names Judaea and Samaria), and Gaza. Israel's victory gave rise to another exodus of Palestinians, with more than 250,000 people fleeing to the eastern bank of the Jordan River. However, roughly 600,000 Palestinians remained in the West Bank and 300,000 in Gaza. Thus the three million Israeli Jews came to rule some 1.2 million Arabs, which included the 300,000 already living in the State of Israel. Moreover, a movement developed among Israelis who advocated settling the occupied territories—particularly the West Bank—as part of the Jewish patrimony in the Holy Land. Several thousand Israeli Jews settled in the territories in the decade following the war.

In the years following the 1967 war, circumstances changed dramatically for Israeli Arabs. As a result of their resumed contact with the Palestinians of the West Bank and the Gaza Strip, they began to recover from their long period of inactivity. Following the October (Yom Kippur) War of 1973, Arab Israelis played a greater role in Israeli institutions. They also were significantly affected by Israel's economic prosperity. By the 1980s the Arab economy had gained some autonomy, as Arabs moved from unskilled work to business ownership.

The PLO's Rise as a Revolutionary Force

Throughout the 1970s and '80s the PLO, dominated by Fatah, acted as a state in the making, launching frequent military attacks on Israel. The strategy of armed struggle had been inaugurated as early as the 1950s, and, indeed, guerrilla raids against military and civilian targets in Israel had been a factor leading to the Suez Crisis of 1956 and the 1967 war. However, after 1967 Fatah launched a new wave of violent activities, and the Palestinian guerrilla groups, under the umbrella of the PLO, emerged as an element of major importance in the Middle East. The 1967 war had discredited Nasser's pan-Arabism, and Fatah quickly permeated and mobilized the reunited Palestinian population, providing social services and organizations. One result was an escalating cycle of raids and reprisals between the Palestinian guerrillas and Israel; guerrilla attacks on Israeli occupation forces and terror attacks on Israeli civilians (defended by the PLO until renounced by 'Arafāt in 1988) became a key element in the struggle against Israel.

The PLO's Struggle for Palestinian Autonomy

Although generally recognized as the symbol of the Palestinian national movement, the PLO lacked organizational cohesion. It championed Palestinian distinctiveness and autonomy, but circumstances forced the leadership to remain somewhat distant from the lives of Palestinians. This made it difficult to impose a unified policy. A major problem for the PLO was gaining autonomy in order to pursue Palestinian interests, especially since the effort to do so inevitably brought the organization into conflict with the Arab states in which Palestinians lived.

PALESTINIANS AND THE PLO IN JORDAN

Within Jordan an understanding was reached whereby the royal government allowed the Palestinian guerrillas independent control of their own bases in the Jordan Valley, but relations between the government and the guerrillas remained uneasy. The guerrillas suspected King Hussein—who had to face the damage inflicted upon his country by Israeli reprisals—of preparing to reach a direct settlement with Israel at their expense.

Tensions between the Jordanian army loyal to King Hussein and the Palestinian guerrillas erupted in a brief but bloody civil war in September 1970 that became known as "Black September." On September 6–9 the PFLP hijacked to a Jordanian airstrip three airliners (American, Swiss, and British) with a total of more than 300 people aboard. The hijackers threatened to destroy the aircraft, with the passengers aboard, unless Palestinian guerrillas detained in Europe and Israel were released. All the passengers were freed by September 30, when the PFLP secured its main demands (after destroying the airliners). Full warfare ensued when the Jordanian army moved against the guerrillas.

By September 17 the army was fighting the guerrillas in Amman and in northern Jordan, where the guerrillas were reinforced by Syria-based armoured units of the Palestine

Liberation Army—a body ostensibly part of the PLO but in fact controlled by Syria. Hostilities formally ended on September 25, with the guerrillas still in control of their northern strongholds. Total casualties were variously estimated at 1,000 to 5,000 people killed and up to 10,000 injured. In 1971, however, the fighting resumed, and the Jordanian army established full control over the whole country and crushed the Palestinian military. From that point on, the king and the PLO were deeply suspicious of each other, and the majority of Palestinians holding Jordanian citizenship, especially those living on the West Bank under Israeli control, became highly critical of the king and his policies.

PALESTINIANS AND THE PLO IN LEBANON

Driven from Jordan, the PLO intensified its activities in Lebanon. The presence of more than 235,000 Palestinians was a source of tension and conflict in Lebanon, as it had been in Jordan. Palestinians had few rights, and most worked for low wages in poor conditions. Palestinian guerrillas continued to carry out attacks against Israel. Israel countered with raids, primarily into southern Lebanon. The Lebanese government sought to restrict the activities of the Palestinian guerrillas, which led to sporadic fighting between the Lebanese army and the guerrillas.

In 1973 the Palestinian movement suffered a severe blow from an Israeli commando attack in Beirut in April that killed three of its leaders. Following the attack, the Lebanese army assaulted guerrilla bases and refugee camps throughout the country. An agreement was reached requiring the Palestinians to limit their activities to border areas near Israel and refugee camps near urban centres. After 1973 many Palestinians from Lebanon and Jordan moved to the increasingly prosperous and labour-hungry Arab oil states, such as Kuwait and Saudi Arabia.

INTERNATIONAL RECOGNITION

The PLO made important gains in its international relations during the 1970s. By the end of the decade the organization had representatives in more than 80 countries. On Sept. 22, 1974, the UN General Assembly, overriding strong Israeli objections, included on its agenda for the first time the "Palestine question" as a separate subject for debate rather than as part of the general question of the Middle East. On November 13 the assembly heard 'Arafāt plead for the Palestinian people's national rights.

International recognition of the PLO had important repercussions within the Arab camp. At an Arab summit conference held in Rabat, Morocco, on Oct. 26–28, 1974, King Ḥussein accepted a resolution stating that any "liberated" Palestinian territory "should revert to its legitimate Palestinian owners under the leadership of the PLO."

PLO leader Yāsir 'Arafāt addresses the United Nations General Assembly in 1974. AFP/Getty Images

The Rabat decision was denounced by the more radical "rejection front," composed of the PFLP, the PFLP–GC, the pro-Iraq Arab Liberation Front, and the Front for the Popular Palestinian Struggle, which sought to regain all of Palestine. Although the decision was recognized as enhancing the less extreme position of the PLO elements led by 'Arafāt, the United States continued adamantly to refuse to recognize or deal with the PLO so long as the PLO refused to recognize Israel's right to exist.

PALESTINIANS AND THE CIVIL WAR IN LEBANON

Palestinian guerrilla activity against Israel in 1975 was largely confined to the southern Lebanese border area, where it provoked heavy Israeli attacks from air, land, and sea against Palestinian refugee camps that the Israelis alleged were being used as guerrilla bases. Israeli raids, however, were overshadowed by growing civil strife in Lebanon that developed along Muslim-Christian lines. Civil war between the militias of Lebanon's sectarian groups erupted in 1975, bringing 15 years of bloodshed, in which more than 100,000 people were killed. The presence of Palestinians was a factor contributing to the civil war, and the war proved disastrous for them.

The PLO initially tried to stay out of the fighting, but by the end of 1975 groups within the overall organization, particularly the "rejection front" groups, were being drawn into an alliance with the Muslim and leftist groups fighting against the Christians. Fighting broke out throughout the country during the first half of January 1976 as Christian forces, foremost the right-wing Maronite Phalange, blockaded the Palestinian refugee camps, and the Palestinian forces and their Lebanese allies responded by attacking Christian villages on the coast. Intense fighting continued, and the PLO, in spite of all efforts, proved unable to protect the Palestinian population. In August, after a two-month siege, Christian forces killed an estimated 2,000 to 3,000 Palestinians in the Tall al-Za'tar camp northeast of Beirut. A peace agreement was negotiated in October 1976. The settlement provided for the creation of a 30,000-member Arab Deterrent Force (ADF), a cease-fire throughout the country, withdrawal of forces to positions held before April 1975, and implementation of a 1969 agreement limiting Palestinian guerrilla operations in Lebanon.

Although the Palestinian guerrillas suffered heavy losses in the Lebanese civil war, they continued to mount attacks against Israel in the late 1970s. Israel again responded with raids into southern Lebanon. In September 1977 Israeli troops crossed into southern Lebanon to support right-wing Christian forces. On March 11, 1978, a Palestinian raid into Israel killed three dozen civilian tourists and wounded some 80 others, and Israel invaded southern Lebanon three days later (Operation Litani). On March 19 the UN Security Council passed resolution 425, calling for Israel to withdraw and establishing the UN Interim Force in Lebanon (UNIFIL). The Israelis withdrew their forces only partially and continued to occupy a strip of Lebanese territory along the southern frontier, in violation of this resolution. They had been only partly successful in their aim of destroying Palestinian guerrillas and their bases south of the Līṭānī River. Several hundred of the Palestinian guerrillas had been killed, but most of them had escaped northward. Estimates of civilian casualties ranged from 1,000 to 2,000.

The PLO in the Occupied Territories

Under the Likud Party government of the late 1970s and early '80s, Israel's settlements in the West Bank grew dramatically, as part of a new Likud policy to maintain strategic dominance in the area. The growth in settlements was accompanied by an increase in Israeli control over the territories, and large parts of those territories were incorporated into Israel's infrastructure. As this occupation solidified, many local Palestinian leaders turned to building social organizations, labour unions, and religious, educational, and political institutions.

The PLO responded by making its presence increasingly felt in the occupied territories, building its own youth groups, providing families with economic assistance, and putting in place a rival political infrastructure that made it possible for PLO-supported candidates to win in the municipal elections of 1976. By the early 1980s the PLO had set up an extensive bureaucratic structure that provided health, housing, educational, legal, media, and labour services for Palestinians both inside and outside the camps. Israeli and Jordanian attempts to encourage alternatives to the PLO failed in the 1980s. Active opposition to Israeli control in the West Bank spread, while frequent demonstrations, strikes, and other incidents occurred, particularly among students.

NEGOTIATIONS, VIOLENCE, AND INCIPIENT SELF-RULE

The late 1970s was a period of more active negotiation on Arab-Israeli disputes. The Arab states supported Palestinian participation in an overall settlement providing for Israeli withdrawal from areas occupied since the 1967 war and establishing a Palestinian state in the West Bank and the Gaza Strip. The U.S. position toward the Palestinians showed signs of softening. In March 1977 U.S. Pres. Jimmy Carter spoke of the need for a Palestinian homeland, and he later stated that it was essential for the Palestinians to take part in the peace process. The Israeli cabinet continued to reject the participation of the PLO in the peace process but agreed not to look too closely at the background of Palestinians who might become members of delegations from Arab countries.

THE CAMP DAVID ACCORDS AND THE PLO

In November 1977 the Egyptian president, Anwar el-Sādāt, initiated peace negotiations that led to the agreement known as the Camp David Accords in September 1978 and to the Egyptian-Israeli peace treaty signed on March 26, 1979. Provisions of the accords (named for Camp David, Md., U.S., where they were negotiated) included the establishment of a self-governing authority in the West Bank and the Gaza Strip and a transitional period of not more than five years, during which time Israel, Jordan, Egypt, and the Palestinians would undertake talks on final status.

As U.S. Pres. Jimmy Carter looks on, Egyptian Pres. Anwar el-Sādāt (left) *shakes hands with Israeli Premier Menachem Begin* (right), *during peace talks at Camp David in 1978.* Karl Schumacher/AFP/Getty Images

During the time of the peace negotiations, the Soviet Union recognized the PLO as the sole legitimate representative of the Palestinians, and in 1981 extended formal diplomatic recognition. The countries of western Europe announced their support of PLO participation in peace negotiations in June 1980. The PLO continued to seek diplomatic recognition from the United States, but the Carter administration honoured a secret commitment the former U.S. secretary of state Henry Kissinger made to Israel not to deal with the PLO so long as it declined to renounce terrorism and to recognize Israel's right to exist.

THE DISPERSAL OF THE PLO FROM LEBANON

The Likud Party government of Israel viewed the possibility of peace and compromise with suspicion. On June 6, 1982, Israel, claiming that it intended to end attacks on its territory (although a cease-fire had been in effect since July 1981) and aiming to dislodge the PLO and encourage the installation of a Lebanese government friendly to Israel, launched an invasion of Lebanon. PLO and Syrian forces were defeated by Israeli troops, and the remaining PLO forces were contained in West Beirut. After a lengthy siege and bombardment by Israel in July and August 1982, some 11,000 Palestinian fighters were allowed to leave Beirut for various destinations, under international guarantees for their own safety and that of their civilian dependents. In spite of these guarantees, however, after Israeli troops had occupied West Beirut, the Phalangists, Israel's rightist Lebanese allies, were allowed by Israeli forces into the Beirut refugee camps of Sabra and Shatila, where they massacred hundreds (estimates vary between 700 and 3,000) of Palestinian and Lebanese civilians.

Although not all PLO guerrillas were forced to leave Lebanon, the PLO infrastructure in the southern part of the country was destroyed, and 'Arafāt's departure from Beirut to northern Lebanon marked the effective end of the PLO's military and political presence in the country. Ultimately, the new government of Lebanon came under the sway of Syria. The dispersal of the PLO from Lebanon significantly weakened the organization's military strength and political militancy. It was unable to operate freely from any of the countries bordering Israel. 'Arafāt and the other PLO leaders were also threatened by the emergence within Fatah of a faction encouraged by Syria. In December 1983 'Arafāt was driven out of northern Lebanon by the Syrians and their protégés inside the PLO.

After having established himself near Tunis, Tun., 'Arafāt turned once again to diplomatic initiatives. He sought Egyptian and Jordanian support against Syria. He also looked to King Ḥussein as an intermediary for negotiations with the United States and Israel that might lead to a Palestinian ministate on the West Bank within a Jordan-Palestine confederation—an idea that had been favoured by the dominant factions in the PLO since the early 1980s. This policy was expressed most concretely in the meeting of the Palestine National Council in Amman in November 1984, the first time it had met there since Jordan had crushed the PLO armed forces in 1970.

YEARS OF MOUNTING VIOLENCE

Violence escalated from the mid-1980s onward. Rejectionist elements within the PLO renewed their activities, attracting worldwide attention. In October 1985 members of the Palestine Liberation Front, a small faction within the PLO headed by Abū 'Abbās, hijacked an Italian cruise ship, the *Achille Lauro*, and murdered one of its passengers. Following an Israeli bombing attack on PLO headquarters near Tunis several days before the hijacking, 'Arafāt moved some departments to Ṣaddām Ḥussein's Iraq. Lebanese Shī'ite Muslim groups fought the PLO to stop its reemergence as an armed rival for supremacy in the chaotic situation prevalent in West Beirut and southern Lebanon. West Bank Arabs demonstrated and engaged in strikes in late 1986.

In Israel several new developments strengthened Arab feelings of alienation from the Jewish majority. Ultranationalists increased their demands for more Jewish settlements and the annexation of the West Bank and advocated the forceful removal of the Palestinian Arabs from the occupied territories. The Israeli parliament passed a bill in 1985 banning any political party that endangered state security—i.e., any party that was anti-Zionist. This reinforced the feeling of most Israeli Arabs that no legal political party could adequately reflect their national, economic, and political views, although the only party actually banned was the anti-Arab Kach Party. Israelis—especially West Bank settlers—became more antagonistic and militant toward Palestinians as armed attacks against Israel and Israelis living abroad increased in number. Throughout 1986–87 attacks by Arabs on Israeli settlers and by Israeli settlers on Arabs mounted. By 1988 more than half of the land in the West Bank and about one-third of the land in the Gaza Strip had been transferred to Jewish control, and the Israeli population of the West Bank—mostly concentrated in 15 metropolitan satellites of Tel Aviv–Yafo and Jerusalem—had reached about 100,000.

By the late 1980s a whole generation of Palestinian youth had grown up under Israeli occupation. Nearly three-fourths of Palestinians were younger than 25 years of age. Their political status was uncertain, their civil rights diminished, and their economic status low and dependent on Israel's economy. Between 100,000 and 120,000 Palestinians crossed daily from the occupied territories into Israel to work. They did not have much faith in Arab governments, nor did they place strong trust in the PLO, which, although still a powerful symbol of Palestinian aspirations, had not succeeded by either diplomatic or military efforts to win Palestinian self-determination. Remittances to family members left behind from those hundreds of thousands who had migrated to Jordan and the Persian Gulf states for work in the 1960s and '70s were reduced drastically as the economies of many Middle Eastern countries were hit by falling oil prices. Increasingly, Palestinians came to rely on their own efforts.

THE *INTIFĀḌAH*

When the Palestinians saw no improvement in effective support of their aspirations from other countries and no likely favourable change coming from the Israelis, they engaged, throughout 1987, in small-scale demonstrations, riots, and occasional violence directed against Israelis. The Israeli authorities responded with university closings, arrests, and deportations. Large-scale riots and demonstrations broke out in the Gaza Strip in early December and continued for more than five years thereafter. This uprising, which became known as the *intifāḍah* (Arabic: "shaking off"), inspired a new era in Palestinian mass mobilization. Masked young demonstrators turned to throwing stones at Israeli troops, and the soldiers responded by shooting and arresting them. Women, and women's organizations, were prominent. The persistent disturbances, initially spontaneous, before long came under the leadership of the Unified National Command of the Uprising, which had links to the PLO. The PLO soon incorporated the Unified Command, but not before the local leaders had pushed 'Arafāt to abandon formally his commitment to armed struggle and to accept Israel and the notion of a two-state solution to the conflict.

One group, Ḥamās, challenged the authority of the secular nationalist movement, especially inside Gaza, and sought to take over the leadership of the *intifāḍah*. Ḥamās was an underground wing of the Muslim Brotherhood, which had built up a network of religious, educational, and charitable institutions in the occupied territories, in addition to establishing an armed wing known as the Sheikh 'Izz al-Dīn al-Qassām Brigades (named for the nationalist leader killed by the British in 1935). Ḥamās rejected any accommodation with Israel.

Ḥamās

Ḥamās (an acronym of Ḥarakat al-Muqāwamah al-Islāmiyyah; English: Islamic Resistance Movement) is a militant Palestinian Islamic movement in the West Bank and Gaza Strip that is dedicated to the destruction of Israel and the creation of an Islamic state in Palestine. Founded in 1987, Ḥamās opposed the 1993 peace accords between Israel and the PLO.

From the late 1970s, Islamic activists connected with the pan-Islamic Muslim Brotherhood established a network of charities, clinics, and schools and became active in the territories (the Gaza Strip and West Bank) occupied by Israel after the 1967 war. In Gaza they were active in many mosques, while their activities in the West Bank generally were limited to the universities. The Muslim Brotherhood's activities in these areas were generally nonviolent, but a number of small groups in the occupied territories began to call for jihad, or holy war, against Israel. In December 1987, at the beginning of the Palestinian *intifāḍah* movement against Israeli occupation, Ḥamās (which also is an Arabic word meaning "zeal") was established by members of the Muslim Brotherhood and religious factions of the PLO, and the new organization quickly acquired a broad following. In its 1988 charter, Ḥamās maintained that Palestine is an Islamic homeland that can never be surrendered to non-Muslims and that waging holy war to wrest control of Palestine from Israel is a religious duty for Palestinian Muslims. This position brought it into conflict with the PLO, which in 1988 recognized Israel's right to exist.

Ḥamās's armed wing, the ʿIzz al-Dīn al-Qassām Forces, began a campaign of terrorism against Israel. Israel responded by imprisoning the founder of Ḥamās, Shaykh Aḥmad Yāsīn, in 1991 and arresting and deporting hundreds of Ḥamās activists. Ḥamās denounced the 1993 peace agreement between Israel and the PLO and, along with the Islamic Jihad group, subsequently intensified its terror campaign using suicide bombers. The PLO and Israel responded with harsh security and punitive measures, although PLO chairman Yāsir ʿArafāt, seeking to include Ḥamās in the political process, appointed Ḥamās members to leadership positions in the Palestinian Authority (PA). The collapse of peace talks between Israelis and Palestinians in September 2000 led to an increase in violence that came to be known as the Aqṣā *intifāḍah*. That conflict was marked by a degree of violence unseen in the first *intifāḍah*, and Ḥamās activists further escalated their attacks on Israelis and engaged in a number of suicide bombings in Israel itself.

In early 2005 Mahmoud Abbas, president of the PA, and Israeli Prime Minister Ariel Sharon announced a suspension of hostilities as Israel prepared to withdraw troops from some Palestinian territories. After much negotiation, Ḥamās agreed to the cease-fire, although sporadic violence continued. In the 2006 elections for the Palestinian Legislative Council, Ḥamās won a surprise victory over Fatah, capturing the majority of seats. The two groups eventually formed a coalition government, though clashes between Ḥamās and Fatah forces in the Gaza Strip intensified, prompting Abbas to dissolve the Ḥamās-led government and declare a state of emergency in June 2007. Ḥamās was left in control of the Gaza Strip, while a Fatah-led emergency cabinet had control of the West Bank.

Later that year Israel declared the Gaza Strip under Ḥamās a hostile entity and approved a series of sanctions that included power cuts, heavily restricted imports, and border closures. Ḥamās attacks on Israel continued, as did Israeli attacks on the Gaza Strip. After months of negotiations, in June 2008 Israel and Ḥamās agreed to implement a truce scheduled to last six months; however, this was threatened shortly thereafter as each accused the other of violations, which escalated in the last months of the agreement. On December 19 the truce officially expired amid accusations of violations on both sides. Broader hostilities erupted shortly thereafter as Israel, responding to sustained rocket fire, mounted a series of air strikes across the region—among the strongest in years—meant to target Ḥamās. After a week of air strikes, Israeli forces initiated a ground campaign into the Gaza Strip amid calls from the international community for a cease-fire. Following more than three weeks of hostilities—in which perhaps more than 1,000 were killed and tens of thousands left homeless—Israel and Ḥamās each declared a unilateral cease-fire.

TACTICS AND TOLLS

The tactics of the *intifāḍah* were highly sophisticated. Union-organized strikes, commercial boycotts and closures, and demonstrations were carried out in one part of the territories, and then, after Israel had reestablished its local power there, they were transferred to a previously quiescent area. Palestinian refugee camps provided major centres for the resistance, but Palestinian Arabs living in more affluent circumstances also participated, and some Israeli Arabs showed their sympathy with the goals of the uprising. During its first year more than 300 Palestinians were killed, more than 11,500 wounded (nearly two-thirds of whom were under 15 years of age), and many more arrested. Israel closed universities and schools, destroyed houses, and imposed curfews—yet it was unable to quell the uprising. By mid-1990 the International Red Cross estimated that more than 800 Palestinians had been killed by Israeli security forces, more than 200 of whom were under the age of 16. Some 16,000 Palestinians were in prison. By contrast, fewer than 50 Israelis had been killed. Some hundreds of Palestinians in the occupied territories, accused of being collaborators with Israel, were killed by their compatriots. Political paralysis gripped Israel.

PLO DECLARATION OF INDEPENDENCE

'Arafāt sought to establish himself as the only leader who could unite and speak for the Palestinians, and in mid-1988 he took the diplomatic initiative. At the 19th session of the PNC, held near Algiers on Nov. 12–15, 1988, he succeeded in having the council issue a declaration of independence for a state of Palestine in the West Bank and Gaza Strip. 'Arafāt proclaimed the state (without defining its borders) on November 15. Within days more than 25 countries (including the Soviet Union and Egypt but excluding the United States and Israel) had extended recognition to the government-in-exile.

The final weeks of 1988 opened a new chapter in Palestinian-Israeli relations. In December 'Arafāt announced that the PNC recognized Israel as a state in the region and condemned and rejected terrorism in all its forms—including state terrorism, the PLO's term for Israel's actions. He addressed a special meeting of the UN General Assembly convened at Geneva and proposed an international peace conference under UN auspices. He publicly accepted UN resolutions 242 and 338, thereby recognizing, at least implicitly, the State of Israel. In spite of their ambiguities, UN Resolution 242 (1967), which encapsulated the principle of land for peace, and UN Resolution 338 (1973), which called for direct negotiations, were regarded by both parties as the starting points for negotiations. Although Israeli Prime Minister Yitzhak Shamir stated that he was still not prepared to negotiate with the PLO, the U.S. government announced that it would open dialogue with the PLO.

The Move Toward Self-Rule

The approaching end of the Cold War left the Palestinians diplomatically isolated, as did PLO support for Iraqi Pres. Ṣaddām Ḥussein, who had invaded Kuwait in August 1990 but was defeated by a U.S.-led alliance in the Persian Gulf War (1990–91). Funds from Saudi Arabia, Kuwait, and the Persian Gulf states dried up. The Palestinian community in Kuwait, which had consisted of about 400,000 people, was reduced to a few thousand. Economic hardship was compounded by the fact that, during the continuing conflict along the Lebanese border and in the occupied territories, Israel imposed severe travel restrictions on Palestinian day labourers. The overall result was loss of jobs, loss of morale, and loss of support for the PLO leadership in Tunis.

However, prospects for a settlement of the outstanding issues between the Palestinians and Israel became significantly altered by several factors: the convening of an international peace conference between Israeli and Arab delegates (including Palestinians from the occupied territories as part of a joint Jordanian-Palestinian delegation) at Madrid in October 1991, sponsored by the United States and the Soviet Union (after December 1991, Russia); the dissolution of the Soviet Union in December; and the replacement, in the Israeli general elections of June 1992, of Shamir and the Likud-bloc government with a Labour Party government that was committed to implementing Palestinian autonomy within a year.

Although progress at the Madrid peace conference was discouraging, secret meetings held in Norway from January 1993 between PLO and Israeli officials produced an understanding known as the Oslo Accords. On this basis, on Sept. 13, 1993, the PLO and Israel signed a historic Declaration of Principles in Washington, D.C. It included mutual recognition and terms whereby governing functions in the West Bank and Gaza would be progressively handed over to a Palestinian Council for an interim period of five years, during which time Israel and the Palestinians would negotiate a permanent peace treaty to settle on the final status of the territories.

In spite of acts of violence committed by extremist groups on both sides attempting to sabotage the peace process, the Israelis completed their withdrawal from the West Bank town of Jericho and parts of the Gaza Strip in May 1994. On July 1 'Arafāt entered Gaza in triumph. Four days later he swore in members of the Palestinian Authority (PA) in Jericho, which by the end of the year had assumed control of education and culture, social welfare, health, tourism, and taxation.

PLO Chairman Yāsir 'Arafāt is carried triumphantly on the shoulders of supporters during the celebration marking Palestinian self-rule in the Gaza Strip, July 1994. Manoocher Deghati/AFP/Getty Images

Violence and irreconcilable demands by radical elements in the populations of both sides obstructed talks between the PLO and the Israeli government. Nonetheless, on Sept. 28, 1995, 'Arafāt and Israeli Prime Minister Yitzhak Rabin and Foreign Minister Shimon Peres signed an agreement in Washington providing for the expansion of Palestinian self-rule in the West Bank and for elections of a chairman and a legislative council of the PA. The PA would gain control over six large West Bank towns (Janīn, Nāblus, Ṭūlkarm, Qalqīlyah, Ramallah, and Bethlehem) as well as control over most of Hebron. Israel would also gradually redeploy from some 440 villages, which would come under Palestinian rule. Security for those areas would rest with the Palestinian police, although Israeli military forces would be guaranteed freedom of movement throughout the area from which Israel redeployed. Reaffirming the commitment made in the 1993 peace accord, permanent-status negotiations were to be concluded by 1999.

In October 1995, as West Bank villages, towns, and cities were handed over to the PA, right-wing religious and extremist nationalist Israelis stepped up their rhetoric against Rabin and the peace process. On Nov. 4, 1995, Israelis were stunned when Rabin was assassinated by a Jewish extremist. Peres, Rabin's successor, quickly expressed his determination to continue the planned Israeli deployments.

Elections were held in PA-administered areas in January 1996, in which about three-fourths of Palestinians of the West Bank and Gaza voted. 'Arafāt secured nearly nine-tenths of the vote and assumed the presidency of the PA in February. He also remained chairman of the PLO. Fatah won 55 seats in the 88-seat legislative council. Ḥamās, however, did not participate in the election and continued its violent opposition to the peace process. The

progress toward peace was further cast into doubt when
Benjamin Netanyahu, right-wing leader of the Likud
Party, was elected prime minister of Israel in May 1996.
Netanyahu left office following defeat at the hands of the
Labour Party led by Ehud Barak in May 1999. Although
Netanyahu reached some accords with the Palestinians,
his term in office was marked by increasing mistrust
between the two sides.

Subsequent events, however, were a disappointment to
all concerned, as a number of negotiating deadlines passed
without an agreement. Notable among these was the May
1999 date set as a deadline for a third stage of Israeli military redeployments, an end of the interim period, and
a completion of "permanent status" talks on the most
contentious issues—such as the status of Jerusalem, the
return of refugees, the presence of Israeli settlements in
the occupied territories, and the issue of Palestinian sovereignty and statehood.

Also, after a decade of negotiating, eight of those years
following the signing of the Declaration of Principles, less
than one-fifth of the West Bank (in 15 isolated segments)
and about two-thirds of the Gaza Strip had reverted to
full Palestinian control. The rest remained under Israeli
military occupation (combined with PA civil administration in some areas). The number of Israelis living in West
Bank settlements (that now exceeded 150) had grown by
some 80,000 in that period, and more Arab land had been
confiscated in the occupied territories for expanding settlements and for constructing bypass roads reserved solely
for use by Israelis. Further, the gross domestic product per
capita in Palestinian areas had actually declined in the nine
years after the Madrid Peace Conference, Israel restricted
the movement of Palestinians (and closed Jerusalem to
West Bank and Gaza Strip Palestinians beginning in 1991),
and accusations were widespread of corruption within

the PA and of human rights abuses by its leaders. All of this made life for most residents of PA-controlled areas worse, in many respects, than it had been before the peace process.

An Israeli-Palestinian summit meeting sponsored by the United States in July 2000 failed to resolve these outstanding issues and led only to an increasingly strained situation. In the aftermath of this summit, a visit to Jerusalem's Al-Ḥaram al-Sharīf (the Temple Mount) in September by Likud leader Ariel Sharon—reviled by Palestinians for his role in the 1982 Sabra and Shatila massacres—was the spark that set off a conflagration. The visit was followed by demonstrations near Al-Aqṣā Mosque the next day, in which Israeli security forces killed and wounded dozens of Palestinian demonstrators. That was the signal for a renewed uprising, which reached a level of violence unseen in the first *intifāḍah*—more than 1,000 died in its first 18 months, the overwhelming majority of them Palestinian civilians—and which engulfed the still largely occupied West Bank and Gaza Strip.

Thereafter, suicide bomb attacks by Palestinians in Israeli cities increased. Large numbers of Israelis, most of them civilians, were killed and wounded, and Israeli attacks on PA targets (most located within population centres) raised the already high casualty rate among the Palestinian populace. In the spring of 2002 Israeli troops reoccupied all the towns and cities of the West Bank, reclaiming security control from the PA and tightening restrictions on movement that had earlier been placed on Palestinian residents of the West Bank and Gaza Strip. Negotiations reached a complete impasse, and the future of the occupied territories, and of relations between Palestinians and Israelis, became increasingly uncertain. Sharon, blaming 'Arafāt for instigating the attacks against Israel, confined 'Arafāt to his compound in Ramallah in 2001.

In 2003 the PA established the office of prime minister in an effort to circumvent 'Arafāt and restart the peace process with Israel. 'Arafāt installed Mahmoud Abbas, a moderate, in the post. Abbas called for an end to the *intifāḍah*, but, feeling that his efforts were thwarted by 'Arafāt, Israel, and the United States, he soon resigned. Following 'Arafāt's death in 2004, Abbas was elected chairman of the PLO and president of the PA. In 2005 Israel withdrew soldiers and settlers from parts of the West Bank and from all of the Gaza Strip, which then came under Palestinian control. Although the pullout initially raised hopes for new peace talks, Ḥamās's surprise victory over Fatah in the 2006 elections for the Palestinian Legislative Council and the failure of the two groups to form a coalition government was a source of great domestic and international concern. When clashes between Ḥamās and Fatah forces in the Gaza Strip intensified, Abbas dissolved the Ḥamās-led government and declared a state of emergency in June 2007. As a result of the conflict, Ḥamās was left in control of the Gaza Strip, while Fatah had control of the West Bank. The fracture of the Palestinian leadership—as well as Israel's declaration of the Gaza Strip under Ḥamās a hostile entity and its subsequent blockade of the region—cast the future of Israeli-Palestinian relations in an uncertain light.

ISRAEL: THE LAND AND ITS PEOPLE

I n spite of its small size, about 290 miles (470 km) north-to-south and 85 miles (135 km) east-to-west at its widest point, Israel has four distinct geographic regions—the Mediterranean coastal plain, the hill regions of northern and central Israel, the Great Rift Valley, and the Negev—and a wide range of unique physical features and microclimates.

The population of Israel is primarily composed of Jews, who constitute some three-fourths of the country's total population. Most of the remainder are Palestinian Arabs, who in turn are chiefly Muslim. Other Israeli Arabs are Christians and Druze, although each community accounts for only a small proportion of the overall population. In contrast, Arabs are in the majority in the Gaza Strip and the occupied territory of the West Bank.

RELIEF

Israel's coastal plain is a narrow strip about 115 miles (185 km) long that widens to about 25 miles (40 km) in the south. A sandy shoreline with many beaches borders the Mediterranean coast. Inland to the east, fertile farmland is giving way to growing agricultural settlements and the cities of Tel Aviv and Haifa and their suburbs.

In the north of the country, the mountains of Galilee constitute the highest part of Israel, reaching an elevation of 3,963 feet (1,208 m) at Mount Meron (Arabic: Jebel Jarmaq). These mountains terminate to the east in an escarpment overlooking the Great Rift Valley. The mountains of Galilee are separated from the hills of the Israeli-occupied West Bank to the south by the fertile Plain of Esdraelon, which, running approximately northwest to southeast, connects the coastal plain with the

CHAPTER 3

Great Rift Valley. The Mount Carmel range, which cul-
minates in a peak 1,791 feet (546 m) high, forms a spur
reaching northwest from the highlands of the West Bank,
cutting almost to the coast of Haifa.

Columns of salt rising from the extremely saline waters of the Dead Sea. Peter
Carmichael/ASPECT

The Great Rift Valley, a long fissure in the Earth's crust,
begins beyond the northern frontier of Israel and forms a
series of valleys running generally south, the length of the
country, to the Gulf of Aqaba. The Jordan River, which
marks part of the frontier between Israel and Jordan,
flows southward through the rift from Dan on Israel's
northern frontier, where it is 500 feet (152 m) above sea
level, first into the Hula Valley, then into the freshwater
Lake Tiberias, also known as the Sea of Galilee, which
lies 686 feet (209 m) below sea level. The Jordan continues south along the eastern edge of the West Bank—now
through the Jordan Valley—and finally into the highly
saline Dead Sea, which, at 1,312 feet (400 m) below sea

level, is the lowest point of a natural landscape feature on the Earth's surface. South of the Dead Sea, the Jordan continues through the rift, where it now forms the 'Arava Valley (Hebrew: "Savannah"), an arid plain that extends to the Red Sea port of Elat.

The sparsely populated Negev comprises the southern half of Israel. Arrow-shaped, this flat, sandy desert region narrows toward the south, where it becomes increasingly arid and breaks into sandstone hills cut by wadis, canyons, and cliffs before finally coming to a point where the 'Arava reaches Elat.

DRAINAGE

The principal drainage system comprises Lake Tiberias and the Jordan River. Other rivers in Israel are the Yarqon, which empties into the Mediterranean near Tel Aviv; the Qishon, which runs through the western part of the Plain of Esdraelon to drain into the Mediterranean at Haifa; and a small section of the Yarmūk, a tributary of the Jordan that flows west along the Syria-Jordan border. Most of the country's remaining streams are ephemeral and flow seasonally as wadis. The rivers are supplemented by a spring-fed underground water table that is tapped by wells. Israel has a chronic water shortage, and its hydraulic resources are fully utilized: about three-fourths for irrigation and the remainder for industrial and household water use.

Yarqon River

The Yarqon River (Hebrew: Naḥal Yarqon) is a river in west-central Israel and is the principal perennial stream flowing almost entirely within the country. The river's name is derived from the Hebrew word *yaroq* ("green"); in Arabic, it is known as Nahr Al-'Awjā' ("The

Tortuous River"). The Yarqon rises in springs near Rosh Ha-'Ayin and flows westward for about 16 miles (26 km) to the Mediterranean in northern Tel Aviv–Yafo. It marks the boundary between the Plain of Sharon (north) and the coastal lowlands (south). The seasonal watercourses west of Rosh Ha-'Ayin, which form part of the drainage system, extend eastward into the West Bank. They include the Wadi Shillo (Dayr Ballūṭ) in the east, usually considered by geographers to mark the boundary between historic Judaea and Samaria, and the Wadi Ayyalon (Aijalon) in the southeast. In the valley of the latter, according to the Bible, the moon stood still during Joshua's conquest of the Amorites (Joshua 10).

Until the 1950s the Yarqon was a pleasant stream frequented by boaters; since the construction and expansion of the Yarqon-Negev Project, part of the National Water Plan (1955 and following), the water level has gone down and pollution has increased.

The Yarqon basin was the centre of several 19th and early 20th-century Jewish settlements, including Petaḥ Tiqwa, Bene Beraq, Ramat Gan, and Tel Aviv, that have grown into cities. It was also the site of several important British victories over the Turks in their conquest of Palestine during World War I. At the mouth of the river, in Tel Aviv, a shallow-draft port was built during the prolonged strike of the Arab port workers of Jaffa (1936); after World War II, however, it was abandoned.

Near the river's mouth, adjacent to the campus of Tel Aviv University, are the important archaeological excavations of Tell Qasile.

SOILS

The coastal plain is covered mainly by alluvial soils. Parts of the arid northern Negev, where soil development would not be expected, have windblown loess soils because of proximity to the coastal plain. The soils of Galilee change from calcareous rock in the coastal plain, to Cenomanian and Turonian limestone (deposited from about 99 to 89 million years ago) in Upper Galilee, and to Eocene formations (those dating from about 55 to 35 million years ago) in the lower part of the region. Rock salt and gypsum are abundant in the Great Rift Valley. The southern Negev is mainly sandstone rock with veins of granite.

CLIMATE

Israel has a wide variety of climatic conditions, caused mainly by the country's diverse topography. There are two distinct seasons: a cool, rainy winter (October–April) and a dry, hot summer (May–September). Along the coast, sea breezes have a moderating influence in summer, and the Mediterranean beaches are popular. Precipitation is light in the south, amounting to about 1 inch (25 mm) per year in the 'Arava Valley south of the Dead Sea, while in the north it is relatively heavy, up to 44 inches (1,120 mm) a year in the Upper Galilee region. In the large cities, along the coastal plain, annual precipitation levels average about 20 inches (508 mm) per year. Precipitation occurs on about 60 days during the year, spread over the rainy season. Severe summer water shortages ensue in years when the rains come late or precipitation totals are less than normal.

Average annual temperatures vary throughout Israel based on elevation and location, with the coastal areas adjacent to the Mediterranean Sea having milder temperatures—ranging from the mid-80s F (high 20s C) in August to the low 60s F (mid-10s C) in January—and higher rates of humidity than areas inland, especially during the winter. Likewise, higher elevations, such as Upper Galilee, have cool nights, even in summer, and occasional snows in the winter. However, the coastal city of Elat, in the south, in spite of its proximity to the Red Sea, is closer to the climate of the Jordan and 'Arava valleys and the Negev, which are hotter and drier than the northern coast; there, daytime temperatures reach the low 70s F (low 20s C) in January and may rise as high as 114 °F (46 °C) in August, when the average high is in the low 100s F (low 40s C).

PLANT AND ANIMAL LIFE

Natural vegetation is highly varied, and more than 2,800 plant species have been identified. The original evergreen forests, the legendary "cedars of Lebanon," have largely disappeared after many centuries of timber cutting for shipbuilding and to clear land for cultivation and goat herding. They have been replaced by second-growth oak and

A view of the foothills of Galilee, featuring some of the area's indigenous vegetation. Hemera/Thinkstock

smaller evergreen conifers. The hills are mostly covered by maquis, and wildflowers bloom profusely in the rainy season. Only wild desert scrub grows in the Negev and on the sand dunes of the coastal plain. North of Beersheba, most of the country is under cultivation or is used for hill grazing. Where irrigation is available, citrus groves, orchards of subtropical fruit, and food crops flourish. Millions of trees have been planted through a government reforestation program.

Animal life is also diverse. Mammals include wildcats, wild boars, gazelles, ibex, jackals, hyenas, hares, coneys, badgers, and tiger weasels. Notable among the reptiles are geckos and lizards of the genus *Agama* and vipers such as the carpet, or saw-scaled, viper (*Echis carinatus*). More than 380 species of birds have been identified in the region, including the partridge, tropical cuckoo, bustard, sand grouse, and desert lark. There are many kinds of fish and insects, and locusts from the desert sometimes invade settled areas. Several regions have been set aside as nature reserves, notably parts of the 'Arava in the south and Mount Carmel, Mount Meron, and the remains of the Ḥula Lake and marshes in the north. The Mediterranean coast and the Jordan and 'Arava valleys are important routes for migratory birds.

RELIGIOUS AND ETHNIC GROUPS

Jews constitute about three-fourths of the total population of Israel. Almost all the rest are Palestinian Arabs, of whom most are Muslim; the remaining Arabs are Christians and Druze, who each make up only a small fraction of the total population. Arabs are the overwhelming majority in the Gaza Strip and the occupied territory of the West Bank.

JEWS

The Jewish population is diverse. Jews from eastern and western Europe, the Middle East and North Africa, Central Asia, North America, and Latin America have been immigrating to this area since the late 19th century. Differing in ethnic origin and culture, they brought with them languages and customs from a variety of countries. The Jewish community today includes survivors of the Holocaust, offspring of those survivors, and émigrés escaping anti-Semitism. The revival of Hebrew as a common language and a strong Israeli national consciousness have facilitated the assimilation of newcomers to Israel but not completely eradicated native ethnicities. For example, religious Jews immigrating to Israel generally continue to pray in synagogues established by their respective communities.

Religious Jewry in Israel constitutes a significant and articulate section of the population. As such, it is often at odds with a strong secular sector that seeks to prevent religious bodies and authorities from dominating national life. The two main religious-ethnic groupings are those Jews from central and eastern Europe and their descendants who follow the Ashkenazic traditions and those Jews from the Mediterranean region and North Africa who follow the Sephardic. There are two chief rabbis in Israel, one Ashkenazi and one Sephardi. Tension is frequent between the two groups, largely because of their cultural differences and the social and political dominance of the Ashkenazim in Israeli society. Until recently, it was generally true that the Sephardim tended to be poorer, less educated, and less represented in higher political office than the Ashkenazim.

Ashkenazim and Sephardim

Ashkenazi Jews (from Hebrew *Ashkenaz*, meaning "Germany"; plural Ashkenazim) are any of the Jews who lived in the Rhineland valley and in neighbouring France before their migration eastward to Slavic lands (e.g., Poland, Lithuania, Russia) after the Crusades (11th–13th century). After the 17th-century persecutions in eastern Europe, large numbers of these Jews resettled in western Europe, where they assimilated, as they had done in eastern Europe, with other Jewish communities. In time, all Jews who had adopted the "German rite" synagogue ritual were referred to as Ashkenazim to distinguish them from Sephardic (Spanish rite) Jews. Ashkenazim differ from Sephardim in their pronunciation of Hebrew, in cultural traditions, in synagogue cantillation (chanting), in their widespread use of Yiddish (until the 20th century), and especially in synagogue liturgy.

Today Ashkenazim vastly outnumber Sephardic Jews. All Reform and Conservative Jewish congregations belong to the Ashkenazic tradition.

Sephardi Jews (from Hebrew *Sefarad*, meaning "Spain"; plural Sephardim, also spelled Sefardim) are those Jews, or their descendants, who lived in Spain and Portugal from the Middle Ages until their persecution and mass expulsion from those countries in the last decades of the 15th century. The Sephardim initially fled to North Africa and other parts of the Ottoman Empire, and many of these eventually settled in such countries as France, Holland, England, Italy, and the Balkans. Salonika (Thessaloníki) in Macedonia and the city of Amsterdam became major sites of Sephardic settlement. The transplanted Sephardim largely retained their native Judeo-Spanish language (Ladino), literature, and customs. They became noted for their cultural and intellectual achievements within the Mediterranean and northern European Jewish communities. The Sephardim differ notably from Ashkenazi (German-rite) Jews in preserving Babylonian rather than Palestinian Jewish ritual traditions.

Though the term "Oriental Jews" is perhaps more properly applied to Jews of North Africa and the Middle East who had no ties with either Spain or Germany and who speak Arabic, Persian, or a variant of ancient Aramaic, the designation Sephardim frequently signifies all North African Jews and others who, under the influence of the "Spanish Jews," have adopted the Sephardic rite.

KARAITES

The Karaites are a Jewish sect that emerged in the early Middle Ages. Several thousand members live in Ramla, and more recently in Beersheba and Ashdod. Like other religious minorities, they have their own religious courts and communal organizations. Considered part of Jewish society, they have maintained their separate identity by resisting intermarriage and preserving their religious rites based on the Torah as the sole source of religious law.

SAMARITANS

Samaritans trace their roots to those Jews not dispersed when the Assyrians conquered Israel in the 8th century BCE. About half of the few hundred surviving members of the Samaritan community live near Tel Aviv in the town of Ḥolon. The rest live on Mount Gerizim (Arabic: Jabal Al-Ṭūr), near Nāblus in the West Bank. They preserve their separate religious and communal organizations and speak Arabic but pray in an archaic form of Hebrew. They participate in national life as part of the Jewish section of the population.

ARABS

Arabs constitute the largest single minority in Israel, and though most are Muslims of the Sunni branch, Arab Christians form a significant minority, particularly in the Galilee region in northern Israel. Arabs, whether Christian, Muslim, or Druze, speak a dialect of Levantine Arabic and learn Modern Standard Arabic in school. An increasing number also avail themselves of higher education within Israel's public schools and colleges, and many younger Arabs are now bilingual in Hebrew. Although most Israeli Arabs consider themselves Palestinians, all are full Israeli citizens with political and civil rights that are, with the exception of some limitations on military service, equal to those of Israeli Jews. Many Arabs participate actively in the Israeli political process, and several Arab political parties have members in the Israeli Knesset. In spite of this inclusiveness, however, many Israeli Arabs still see themselves as living in an occupied state, and suspicions and antagonism persist.

MUSLIMS

The overwhelming majority of Israel's Muslims are Arabs. Like all other religious communities, Muslims enjoy considerable autonomy in dealing with matters of personal status. They have separate religious courts for issues such as marriage, divorce, and inheritance. The state oversees their religious institutions. Israel's Bedouin, which form a small proportion of the Arab population, are exclusively Muslim.

CHRISTIANS

Most Christians in Israel are Arabs, and Christian communities in Israel, regardless of ethnicity, have a wide degree of autonomy in religious and communal affairs. The Greek Catholic and Greek Orthodox churches are the largest denominations, and most of them are found in Jerusalem. Apart from the Greek Orthodox church, which has a patriarchate in Jerusalem, each church is dependent to a degree on a supreme hierarch abroad. These communities include Roman Catholics and Uniates (Melchites, Maronites, Chaldean Catholics, Syrian Catholics, and Armenian Catholics). Jerusalem also has a Russian Orthodox community. The Evangelical, Episcopal, and Lutheran churches are small and primarily Arabic-speaking.

DRUZE

The Druze, who live in villages in Galilee and around
Mount Carmel, have traditionally formed a closed,
tight-knit community and practice a secretive religion
founded in 11th-century Fāṭimid Egypt. Though Israeli
Druze maintain contact with coreligionists in Lebanon
and Syria, members of each group adhere to the authority of the country of their residence. Israel has recognized
the Druze as a separate Arab community since 1957, and
Israeli Druze serve in the armed forces. Druze have traditionally been agriculturists, but younger members have
found employment throughout the economy.

OTHER GROUPS

The Bahā'ī faith, a universal religion founded in Iran in the
mid-19th century, is the only religion other than Judaism
to have its world centre in Israel. A teaching centre,
archive building, shrine, and administrative headquarters
are located on Mount Carmel in Haifa. There are a few
hundred adherents in Israel, most of whom are employed
at the centre in Haifa.

The Circassians, who are Sunni Muslims, emigrated
from the Caucasus in the 1870s. They number a few thousand and live in villages in Galilee, preserving their native
language and traditions. Older Circassians speak Arabic as
well as the Circassian language, but members of the younger
generation speak Hebrew. The men serve in the Israeli
armed forces.

SETTLEMENT PATTERNS

Jewish immigration in the 20th century greatly altered the
settlement pattern of the country. The first modern-day

Jewish settlers established themselves on the coastal plain in the 1880s. Later they also moved into the valleys of the interior and into parts of the hill districts, as well as into the Negev. Small cities such as Haifa and Jerusalem grew in size, and the port of Jaffa (Yafo) sprouted a suburb, Tel Aviv, which grew into the largest city in Israel. Jewish immigrants also settled those areas of the coastal plain, the Judaean foothills, and the Jordan and 'Arava valleys evacuated by Palestinians during the war of 1948, thereby becoming the majority in many areas previously inhabited by Arabs. Although the majority of the Bedouin of the Negev left the region when Israel incorporated the territory, the desert has continued to be largely the domain of the Arab nomads who remained or returned following the end of fighting.

The non-Jewish population is concentrated mainly in Jerusalem (about one-fifth of the residents of the city),

Jews and Palestinians traverse a crowded market place in Jerusalem. Public spaces within the area's "Old City" are shared by people of different ethnicities and faiths. Khaled Desouki/AFP/Getty Images

and in the north, where Arabs constitute a substantial part of the population of Galilee.

Jerusalem, perched high among the Judaean hills, is one of the great cities of the world, with a long history, unique architecture, and rich archeological heritage. Israel claims Jerusalem as its capital, although that status has not received full recognition by the international community. Jerusalem's walled "Old City" is divided into four quarters—Muslim, Jewish, Christian, and Armenian—symbolizing its spiritual significance to the region's major religious and ethnic groups.

RURAL SETTLEMENT

The rural population, defined as residents of settlements with less than 2,000 people, amounts to less than one-tenth of the country's total inhabitants. About one-tenth of the Jewish population is rural, of whom more than half are immigrants who arrived after 1948. The Jewish rural settlements are organized into kibbutzim, which are collective groups voluntarily practicing joint production and consumption; moshavim, which are cooperatives of small holders who practice joint sales and purchases, make common use of machinery, minimize hired labour, and lease national land; and agricultural communities or individually owned farms engaged in private production. The kibbutzim and moshavim pioneered settlement in underdeveloped areas, performed security functions in border areas, and contributed substantially to the country's ability to absorb new immigrants in the early years of the state.

Only a tiny fraction of the Arab population lives in rural areas. Those who do are divided between the Bedouin and residents of small agricultural villages. Many such communities are now defined as urban by the Israeli government because their populations exceed 2,000, in spite of the fact that some residents still engage in agriculture. Before 1948 Jewish and Arab agricultural settlements existed side by side but were largely independent of each other. Since then, however, thousands of Arabs from the Gaza Strip and the Israeli-occupied territory of the West Bank have found employment in Israel in the citrus groves or in industry or as construction labourers. This ready labour pool, together with increased agricultural mechanization, has led to a drop in the number of Jewish agricultural workers. In Arab villages, fewer than half of the adult labourers, both men and women, are engaged in working the land.

There has been a growing tendency among farmers to practice intensive cultivation, to diversify crops, and to shift from small holdings to large farms. Most of the remaining Arab farmers work their own land, although some either lease land or work for Arab or Jewish landlords. Many Bedouin also have abandoned herding for work in towns and cities, establishing residence in permanent settlements that continue to maintain traditional tribal identity.

Kibbutz

A kibbutz (Hebrew: "gathering" or "collective"; plural kibbutzim) is an Israeli collective settlement, usually agricultural and often also industrial, in which all wealth is held in common. Profits are reinvested in the settlement after members have been provided with food, clothing, and shelter and with social and medical services. Adults have private quarters, but children are generally housed and cared for as a group. Cooking and dining are in common. The settlements have edged toward greater privacy with regard to person and property since the formation of Israel in 1948. The kibbutzim, which are generally established on land leased from the Jewish National Fund, convene weekly general meetings at which the kibbutz members determine policy and elect their administrative members.

The first kibbutz was founded at Deganya in Palestine in 1909. Others were created in the following years, and by the early 21st century there were more than 250 kibbutzim in Israel, their total population numbering more than 100,000. The early kibbutzim in Palestine were actually *kevuzot;* these were relatively small collectives that gradually evolved into the larger and more extended collective community known as the kibbutz. The kibbutzim played an important role in the pioneering of new Jewish settlements in Palestine, and their democratic and egalitarian character had a strong influence on early Israeli society as a whole. The kibbutzim still make contributions to Israel's economy and leadership that are disproportionately large when compared with the kibbutzim's relatively small share of the country's population.

URBAN SETTLEMENT

The great majority of the population, both Jewish and Arab, reside in urban areas. As the industrial and service sectors of the economy have grown, the two large conurbations of Tel Aviv–Yafo and Haifa, along the coastal plain, now house more than half of the country's population; Jerusalem and Rishon LeZiyyon are also substantial population centres. The government has made great efforts to prevent the population from becoming overconcentrated in these areas, overseeing in both the north and south the development of new towns occupied largely by the country's most recent immigrants. These towns serve as centres of regional settlement and fulfill specialized economic functions, such as the manufacture of textiles, clothing, machinery, electronic equipment, and computer software. One such place, Beersheba, in the northern Negev, grew from a planned new town founded on a small older settlement in the 1950s into a city, the result of waves of Jewish immigrants from North Africa and the former Soviet Union.

The major urban centres inhabited by Arabs include cities and towns with both Arab and Jewish populations—such as Jerusalem, Haifa, 'Akko, Lod, Ramla, and Yafo—and towns with predominantly Arab populations, including Nazareth in Galilee, where a mainly Jewish suburb is nearly equal in population to the Arab city. Many of the former differences in ways of life between Arabs and Jews are diminishing in towns with mixed populations, even though each group usually lives in different quarters.

DEMOGRAPHIC TRENDS

The most significant demographic issue in Israel since its establishment has been Jewish immigration. In 1948 the Jewish population of Israel was about 670,000; this number increased to more than one million the next year as a result of immigration. Between 1949 and 1997 about 2.35 million Jewish immigrants entered the country; about 700,000 to 750,000 Jews left it, although some later returned. The total number of immigrants includes more than 320,000 Soviet Jews who came to Israel in 1989–91 and continued to arrive at the rate of about 50,000 per year. Nearly 28,000 Ethiopian Jews immigrated in 1990–92, adding to an earlier migration of 11,000 in 1984–85. The largest proportion of Jews trace their roots to Europe (including the former Soviet Union) and North America, though some also hail from Africa (mostly North Africa), Asia, and the Middle East.

More than half of the Arab population fled their homes during the war of 1948, of whom only a small fraction were allowed to return after the end of hostilities. While the

Jewish population has grown more from immigration than from natural increase since that time, the Arab population has grown mainly through high birth rates, which are markedly higher than among Israel's Jews, and through the addition of about 66,000 residents of East Jerusalem, captured from Jordan in 1967 and later annexed by Israel. Overall, the population is youthful, with almost one-third being 15 years old or younger. Life expectancy is among the highest in the world: some 83 years for women and 79 years for men.

THE ISRAELI ECONOMY

The large influx of well-trained and Western-educated European and North American immigrants contributed greatly to a rapid rise in Israel's gross national product (GNP) after 1948. Although most of them had to change occupations, a nucleus of highly skilled labour, in combination with the country's rapid founding of universities and research institutes, facilitated economic expansion. The country obtained large amounts of capital, which included gifts from world Jewry, reparations from the Federal Republic of Germany for Nazi crimes, grants-in-aid from the U.S. government, and capital brought in by immigrants. Israel has supplemented these forms of revenue with loans, commercial credits, and foreign investment.

The goals of Israel's economic policy are continued growth and the further integration of the country's economy into world markets. Israel has made progress toward these goals under difficult conditions, such as a rapid population increase, a boycott by neighbouring Arab countries (except Egypt from 1979 and Jordan from 1994), heavy expenditure on defense, a scarcity of natural resources, high rates of inflation, and a small domestic market that limits the economic savings of mass production. In spite of these obstacles, Israel has achieved a high standard of living for most of its residents, the growth of substantial industrial export and tourism sectors, and world-class excellence in advanced technologies and science-based industry. However, this economic progress has not been uniform. Israeli Arabs are generally at the lower rungs of the economic ladder, and there are substantial economic divisions among Israeli Jews, mainly between the Sephardim and Ashkenazim.

Large influxes of capital have passed through government channels and public organizations and enlarged that sector of the economy that engages in enterprises between the government and private concerns. Government policy dating from the late 1970s, however, has been directed toward privatization. The private, governmental, and, to a limited extent, cooperative sectors all coexist in an economy that supports both the broad objectives of state policy and individual enterprise.

AGRICULTURE AND FISHING

Early Israeli society was strongly committed to expanding and intensifying agriculture in Palestine. As a result, a rural Jewish agrarian sector emerged that included two unique forms of farming communities, the kibbutz and the moshav. Although the rural sector makes up a minority of the total Jewish population, such a large rural populace represents something almost unknown in the Diaspora.

The amount of irrigated land has increased dramatically and, along with extensive farm mechanization, has been a major factor in raising the value of Israel's agricultural production. These improvements have contributed to a great expansion in cultivating citrus and such industrial crops as peanuts (groundnuts), sugar beets, and cotton, as well as vegetables and flowers. Dairying has also increased considerably in importance. Israel produces the major portion of its food supply and must import the remainder.

The main problem facing agriculture is the scarcity of water. Water is diverted through pipelines from the Jordan and Yarqon rivers and from Lake Tiberias to arid areas in the south. Because almost all the country's current water resources have been fully exploited, further agricultural development involves increasing yields from land already irrigated, obtaining more water by cloud

seeding, reducing the amount of evaporation, desaliniz-
ing seawater, and expanding desert farming in the Negev
by drawing on brackish water found underground. Israel
has perfected drip-irrigation methods that conserve water
and optimize fertilizer use.

*Closeup of a drip irrigation system at work in Israel. Water conservation, partic-
ularly as it pertains to agriculture, is a major concern in this arid region.* James
L. Stanfield/National Geographic Image Collection/Getty Images

Only a limited quantity of fish is available off Israel's
Mediterranean and Red Sea coasts, and Israeli trawlers
sail to the rich fishing grounds in the Indian Ocean off
the Ethiopian coast and engage in deep-sea fishing in the
Atlantic Ocean. Inland, fishpond production meets much
of the domestic demand.

RESOURCES AND POWER

Mineral resources include potash, bromine, and magne-
sium, the last two deriving from the waters of the Dead

Sea. Copper ore is located in the 'Arava, phosphates and small amounts of gypsum in the Negev, and some marble in Galilee. Israel began limited petroleum exploitation in the 1950s, and small oil deposits have been found in the northern Negev and south of Tel Aviv; oil pipelines run from the port of Elat to the Mediterranean. Israel continues to import most of its petroleum, however. The country also has reserves of natural gas in the northern Negev northeast of Beersheba and offshore in the Mediterranean.

The country's mining industry supplies local demands for fertilizers, detergents, and drugs and also produces some exports. A plant in Haifa produces potassium nitrate and phosphoric acid for both local consumption and export. Products of the oil refineries at Haifa include polyethylene and carbon black, which are used by the local tire and plastic industries. The electrochemical industry also produces food chemicals and a variety of other commodities.

The power industry is nationalized, and electricity is generated principally from coal- and oil-burning thermal stations. The government has encouraged intensive rural electrification and has provided electricity for agriculture and industry at favourable rates.

The Israel Atomic Energy Commission was established in 1952 and has undertaken a comprehensive survey of the country's natural resources and trained scientific and technical personnel. A small atomic reactor for nuclear research was constructed with American assistance south of Tel Aviv. A second reactor, built in the Negev with French help, is used for military weapons research.

MANUFACTURING

For more than 40 years local demand fueled Israeli industrial expansion, as the country's population grew rapidly

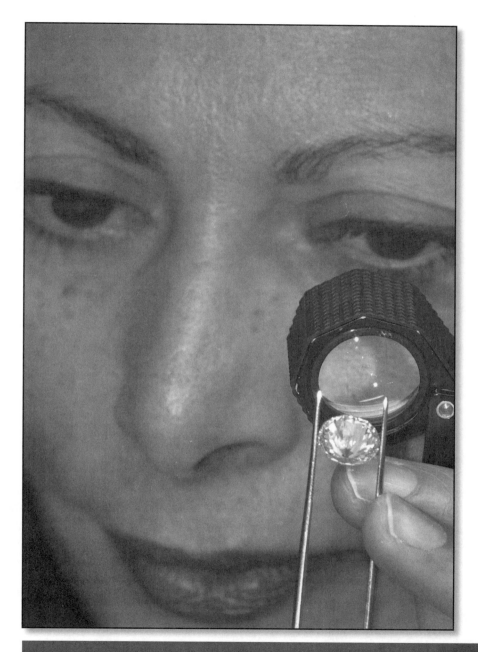

An Israeli diamond dealer inspects a multi-carat stone near Tel Aviv. Israel is a world leader in the diamond trade. David Silverman/Getty Images

and the standard of living rose. Industrial growth has been especially rapid since 1990 in high-technology; science-based industries such as electronics, advanced computer and communications systems, and software have come to command the largest share of overall manufacturing output. Israel's high status in new technologies is the result of its emphasis on higher education and research and development. The government also assists industrial growth by providing low-rate loans from its development budget. The main limitations experienced by industry are the scarcity of domestic raw materials and sources of energy and the restricted size of the local market.

In addition to high-technology items, other principal products include chemicals, plastics, metals, food, and medical and industrial equipment. Israel's diamond-cutting and polishing industry, centred in Tel Aviv, is the largest in the world and is a significant source of foreign exchange. The great majority of industries are privately owned, one exception being the government-run Israel Aircraft Industries, Ltd., a defense and civil aerospace manufacturer. Factories producing military supplies and equipment have expanded considerably since the 1967 war—a circumstance that stimulated the development of the electronics industry.

FINANCE

Israel's central bank, the Bank of Israel, issues currency and acts as the government's sole fiscal and banking agent. Its major function is to regulate the money supply and short-term banking. The Israeli currency was devalued numerous times after 1948, and the new Israeli shekel (NIS) was introduced in September 1985 to replace the earlier Israeli shekel. The government and central bank introduced this measure as part of a successful economic stabilization policy that helped control a rate of inflation that had grown steadily between the 1950s and mid-1980s and had skyrocketed in the 1970s.

Israel has commercial (deposit) banks, cooperative credit institutions, mortgage and investment credit banks, and other financial institutions that are supervised by the central bank. The banking system shows a high degree of specialization. Commercial banks are privately owned and generally are restricted to short-term business. Medium- and long-term transactions, however, are handled by development banks jointly owned by private interests and the government, which cater to the investment needs of different sectors of the economy: agriculture, industry, housing, and shipping. The Tel Aviv Stock Exchange was established in 1953.

TRADE

Access to foreign markets has been vital for further economic expansion. Israel has free trade agreements with the European Union and the United States and is a member of the World Trade Organization. These agreements and Israel's many industrial and scientific innovations have allowed the country to trade successfully in spite of its lack of access to regional markets in the Middle East. A central problem, however, has been the country's large and persistent annual balance-of-trade deficit.

Imports consist mainly of machinery, raw materials (including rough diamonds), capital goods, and food. Exports have increased greatly in value and have become highly diversified, originating in all the major manufacturing sectors and in agriculture. Basic manufactures, machinery and equipment, and chemicals and related products lead the list of exports, and Israel sells fruit (including citrus), vegetables, and flowers throughout

Europe during the off-season. Major trading partners include the United States, Belgium and Luxembourg, and China.

SERVICES

Services on the whole employ more than one-fourth of the Israeli workforce. Tourism has increased significantly and has become an important source of foreign exchange, although its growth at times has been affected by regional strife. Visitors are drawn to Israel's numerous religious, archeological, and historic sites—such as the Western Wall and Dome of the Rock and biblical cities such as Nazareth, and Bethlehem in the West Bank—as well as to its geographic diversity, excellent weather for leisure activities, and links to the Jewish and Palestinian Arab diasporas. There are numerous resorts in the highlands and desert and along the coast, with most tourists coming from the United States, Russia, and European countries.

Western Wall

The Western Wall (Hebrew: Ha-Kotel Ha-Ma'aravi), which is also called the Wailing Wall, is a place of prayer and pilgrimage sacred to the Jewish people. Located in the Old City of Jerusalem, it is the only remains of the Second Temple of Jerusalem, held to be uniquely holy by the ancient Jews and destroyed by the Romans in 70 CE. The authenticity of the Western Wall has been confirmed by tradition, history, and archaeological research; the wall dates from about the 2nd century BCE, though its upper sections were added at a later date.

Because the wall now forms part of a larger wall that surrounds the Muslim Dome of the Rock and Al-Aqṣā Mosque, Jews and Arabs have frequently disputed control of the wall (and, often, right of access

The Western Wall in the Old City of Jerusalem. © Don Smetzer/Stone

to it). This conflict has become particularly heated since the Israeli government took full control of the Old City in the wake of the Six-Day War of June 1967. As it is seen today, the Western Wall measures about 160 feet (50 m) long and about 60 feet (20 m) high; however, it extends much deeper into the earth. Jewish devotions there date from the early Byzantine period and reaffirm the rabbinic belief that "the divine Presence never departs from the Western Wall." Jews lament the destruction of the Temple and pray for its restoration. Such terms as "Wailing Wall" were coined by European travelers who witnessed the mournful vigils of pious Jews before the relic of the sacred Temple. Visitors to the wall have long followed the practice of wedging small slips of paper, upon which prayers and petitions are written, into the cracks between the stones.

Arab and Jewish sources both confirm that, after the Arab capture of Jerusalem in 638 CE, Jews led the conquerors to the site of the Holy Rock and Temple yard and helped clear away the debris.

LABOUR AND TAXATION

The General Federation of Labour in Israel (Histadrut) is the largest labour union and voluntary organization in the country. It once was also one of the largest employers in Israel and owner or joint owner of a wide range of industries, but by the mid-1990s it had sold most of its holdings to private investors. Since 1960 Arab workers have been admitted to the organization with full membership rights. The Manufacturers' Association of Israel and the Farmers' Union represent a large number of the country's employers.

Tax rates in Israel are among the highest in the world, with income, value-added, customs and excise, land, and luxury taxes being the main sources of revenue. The government has gradually raised the proportion of indirect taxes since the late 1950s. Tax reforms in 1985 included a new corporate tax levied on previously untaxed business sectors while slightly reducing direct taxes on individuals.

TRANSPORTATION

Israel has developed a modern, well-marked highway system, and road transport is more significant to the country's commercial and passenger services than transport by rail. Bus companies provide efficient service within and between all cities and towns, supplemented by private taxis and *sheruts*—privately owned and operated shuttles—which run on urban and interurban routes. *Sheruts* also operate on Saturdays, when much of the regular rail and bus service is suspended in observance of the Sabbath.

Shipping is a vital factor both for the economy and in communications with other countries. As a result of the closing of the land frontiers following the Arab blockade of Israel, ocean and air shipping has played a major role in the transportation of supplies. Three modern deep-water ports—Haifa and Ashdod on the Mediterranean and Elat on the Red Sea—are maintained and developed by the Israel Ports and Railways Authority, and are linked to the country by a combined road and rail system. Israel's shipping access routes to both the Atlantic and Indian oceans have stimulated a continuous growth of its merchant fleet and airfreight facilities.

The busy port at Haifa. Shipping is a crucial component of Israel's trade and communications links with other countries. Yoav Lemmer/AFP/Getty Images

The international airport at Lod is the country's largest. Regular flights are maintained by several international airlines, with El Al Israel Airlines Ltd., Israel's national carrier, accounting for the largest share of the traffic. Scheduled domestic aviation and charter aviation abroad is operated by Arkia Israeli Airlines Ltd. Airports at Jerusalem, Tel Aviv, Elat, Rosh Pinna, and Haifa are among those that serve the country's domestic air traffic.

CHAPTER 5

ISRAELI GOVERNMENT AND SOCIETY

I srael does not have a formal written constitution. Instead, its system of government is founded on a series of "basic laws" plus other legislation, executive orders, and parliamentary practice. The country is a democratic republic with a parliamentary system of government headed by a prime minister and involving numerous political parties representing a wide range of political positions.

Israel's lawmaking body, the Knesset, or assembly, is a unicameral, or single-chamber, legislature with 120 members who are elected every four years (or more frequently if a Knesset vote of no confidence in the government results in an early election). Members exercise important functions in standing committees. Hebrew and Arabic, the country's two official languages, are used in all proceedings.

Israel's unicameral legislature, the Knesset, in session, October 2006. David Silverman/Getty Images

On Feb. 16, 1949, the Constituent Assembly—elected in January of that year to prepare the country's constitution—ratified the Transition Law and reconstituted itself as the First Knesset. On the same day, Chaim Weizmann (1874–1952) was elected the first president of Israel. Many of its procedural rules (*takkanoth*) are similar to those of the British House of Commons. Israel did not adopt a formal, written constitution, but it later enacted basic laws on the Knesset (1958), Israeli lands (1960), the term of the president (1964), and the government (1968).

Bills approved as law are published in one series of *Reshumot* ("The Official Gazette: The Book of Laws"). Pending bills are published in two other series.

The country's prime minister is the head of government and is entrusted with the task of forming the cabinet, which is the government's main policy-making and executive body. The cabinet's existence is subject to a vote of confidence in the Knesset. Israel has a strong cabinet, and its members may be—but need not be—members of the Knesset.

The president, who is the head of state, was traditionally elected by the Knesset for a five-year term that could be renewed only once. Beginning in 2000, however, presidents were elected for a single, seven-year term. The president has no veto powers and exercises mainly ceremonial functions but has the authority to appoint certain key national officials, including state comptroller, governor of the Bank of Israel, judges, and justices of the Supreme Court.

The state comptroller—an independent officer elected by the Knesset before being appointed by the president—is responsible only to the Knesset and is the auditor of the government's financial transactions and is empowered to enquire into the efficiency of its activities. The comptroller also acts as a national ombudsman.

Israel's civil service gradually has become a politically neutral and professional body; previously, it tended to be drawn from, and to support, the party in power. The government's extensive responsibilities and functions have acted to enlarge the bureaucracy.

LOCAL AND REGIONAL GOVERNMENT

The country is divided into six districts—Central, Jerusalem, Haifa, Northern, Southern, and Tel Aviv—and thence into subdistricts. Local government consists of municipalities, local councils (for smaller settlements), or regional rural councils. The bylaws of the councils, as well as their budgets, are subject to approval by the Ministry of the Interior. Local government elections are held every five years.

JUSTICE

Municipal, religious, and military courts exercise a jurisdiction almost identical to that exercised by such courts during the period of the Palestine Mandate. Regional labour courts were established in 1969, and matters of marriage and divorce are dealt with by the religious courts of the various recognized communities. Capital punishment has been maintained only for genocide and crimes committed during the Nazi period.

The president appoints judges of the magistrates', district, and supreme courts, and judges hold office until mandatory retirement. The Israeli judiciary is highly independent from political influence.

Israeli law is based on a variety of sources, including Ottoman and British legislation and precedent, religious court opinion, and Israeli parliamentary enactments. The country has convened special investigative panels on unusual occasions—as in the aftermath of the war of 1973 and following the massacre of Palestinians by Christian militiamen in Israeli-controlled sectors of Lebanon in 1982—to issue reports and allocate responsibility among political and military leaders.

POLITICAL PROCESS

National and local elections in Israel are by universal, direct suffrage, with secret balloting. All resident Israeli citizens are enfranchised from age 18, regardless of religion or ethnicity, and candidates for election must be at least 21 years old. For national races, the system of election is by proportional representation, and each party receives the number of Knesset seats that is proportional to the number of votes it receives. If a party's list, for example, receives 5 percent of the vote, the first six persons (5 percent of 120) on that list become members of the Knesset. The parties determine the order of names on their lists.

Israel's party system has traditionally been complex and volatile. Splinter groups are commonly formed, and party alliances often change. Since it is difficult for a single party to win a majority of the seats in the Knesset, government by coalition is common in Israel.

Electoral reform in 1992 brought about two significant changes: direct election of the prime minister—formerly the de facto head of government by dint of being leader of the governing coalition—and primary elections to choose lists of party candidates. The primary system enhanced participatory democracy within the parties, while the prime ministerial ballot increased the power of smaller parties, further splintering the composition of the Knesset and making governing coalitions more difficult to maintain. As a consequence, Knesset representation among the two traditional major parties, Labour and Likud, diminished. In 2001 direct elections for the premiership were repealed, and Israel returned to its earlier practice, in which the governing coalition's leader sits as prime minister. In spite of the change, the two main parties continued to face challenges from minor parties and from new ones such as Kadima, which quickly rose to prominence after being formed in 2005.

Political parties are both secular and religious, with the Jewish secular parties being Zionist and ranging in orientation from left-wing socialist to capitalist, and the religious parties tending to have ethnic appeal (Sephardi or Ashkenazi). There are also several Arab parties.

Israeli citizens take an active interest in public affairs above and beyond membership in political parties. The pattern of Israel's social and economic organization favours participation in trade unions, employers' organizations, and interest groups concerned with state and public affairs.

ISRAELI-OCCUPIED ARAB TERRITORIES

After the 1967 war, Arab territories occupied by Israeli forces were placed under military administration. These included the territory on the west bank of the Jordan River (the West Bank) that had been annexed by Jordan in 1950, the Gaza Strip, the Sinai Peninsula region of Egypt, and the Golan Heights region of Syria. In addition, East Jerusalem (also formerly part of Jordan) was occupied by Israeli forces, and Israel took over administration of the city as a single municipality. In 1967 Israel incorporated

East Jerusalem and adjoining villages and later formally annexed them—actions that have continued to be disputed abroad and hotly contested by Palestinians and neighbouring Arab countries.

In 1978 the Israeli military occupied a strip of Lebanese territory adjoining Israel's northern border, from which it withdrew in 2000. Israel passed legislation effectively annexing the Golan Heights in April 1981, but completed a withdrawal from the Sinai Peninsula in April 1982 after negotiating a peace treaty with Egypt. Likewise, in May 1994, Israel began turning over control of much of the Gaza Strip and parts of the West Bank—including jurisdiction over most of the people in those areas—to the Palestinians in accordance with the provisions set forth in the Cairo Agreement on the Gaza Strip and Jericho signed by the two parties earlier that month. These exchanges of territory were part of a series of agreements, generally referred to as the Oslo Accords, which were initiated by the September 1993 Declaration of Principles on Palestinian Self-Rule. The intent of these agreements was to settle outstanding grievances between the two sides over issues relating to Israeli security and Israel's occupation of Palestinian territory.

The Israelis and the newly formed Palestinian Authority (PA) arranged further exchanges of territory as part of the Interim Agreement on the West Bank and Gaza Strip, signed in September 1995, and the Wye River Memorandum of October 1998. The transfers, executed in stages, actually occurred more slowly than originally agreed, with a number of stages delayed or postponed. In 2002 Israel also began construction on a barrier described as a security measure against suicide attacks. In spite of a 2003 UN General Assembly vote and a nonbinding International Court of Justice ruling condemning the barrier under international law, construction continued.

However, as a result of U.S. negotiations, the barrier, which initially included particularly controversial deviations from the "green line" (the boundary between Israel and the West Bank, as designated by the 1949 cease-fire), was redirected to follow the green line more closely. Beginning in 2004, Israel's Supreme Court also ruled on a number of occasions to change the route of the barrier, responding to appeals from individual Palestinian villages near its course.

Palestinian schoolchildren walk alongside the concrete barrier—being outfitted with barbed wire under armed guard—that separates the West Bank from Israel. Gali Tibbon/AFP/Getty Images

In late 2003 Prime Minister Ariel Sharon proposed a new, unilateral approach, based on the notion that Israel had no partner in peace, entailing a withdrawal from the Gaza Strip and parts of the West Bank. The disengagement plan initially faced significant opposition from within Sharon's own Likud Party but was eventually approved by the Knesset in 2004 amid continued campaigns and resignations opposing it. Nevertheless, in August 2005, as planned, Israel withdrew from the Gaza Strip and dismantled four settlements in the West Bank and turned those areas over to the PA.

SECURITY

The Israel Defense Forces (IDF) is generally regarded by military experts as one of the finest armed forces in the world. IDF doctrine has been shaped since Israel's founding by the country's need to stave off attack from the numerically superior and geographically advantaged forces of its hostile Arab neighbours. This doctrine encompasses the IDF's belief that Israel cannot afford to lose a single war, a goal that it feels can be attained only through a defensive strategy that includes a peerless intelligence community and early warning systems and a well-trained, rapidly mobilized reserve component combined with a strategic capability that consists of a small, highly trained, active-duty force that is able to take the war to the enemy, quickly attain military objectives, and rapidly reduce hostile forces.

An integrated organization encompassing sea, air, and land forces, the IDF consists of a small corps of career officers, active-duty conscripts, and reservists. Military service is compulsory for Jews and Druze, both men and women, and for Circassian men. Muslim and Christian Arabs may volunteer, although because of security concerns, the air force and intelligence corps are closed to minorities. The period of active-duty conscription is three years for men and two for women; this is followed by a decades-long period of compulsory reserve duty (to age 50 for women and age 55 for men). Reservists have 30 to 45 days of military service and training per year, but in times of national emergency reserve duty can be extended indefinitely.

Since the IDF depends on the reserve service of the population to meet manpower requirements, it continues to be mainly a popular militia rather than a professional army. Consequently, civilian-military relations are based firmly on the subordination of the army to civilian control. The chief of staff of the IDF, the country's highest-ranking military officer, is appointed by the government based on the recommendation of the minister of defense, who selects the appointee from ranking IDF officers. Training is a crucial element of Israeli military success, and the IDF administers an extensive network of military schools and colleges for the training of its enlisted personnel and officers. In addition, a special force, the Nahal, combines military and agricultural training and is also responsible for establishing new defense settlements along Israel's borders. Youth battalions conduct premilitary training for young people both in and out of school. The Israeli government also assigns the IDF to provide educational services for recent immigrants whenever the need arises.

The police in Israel are a branch of the Ministry of Public Security and report to a national headquarters commanded by an inspector general. The same ministry administers the country's prison system, which is linked to a system to rehabilitate prisoners following their release. The Border Guard is a military arm of the national police and is responsible for maintaining internal security and combating terrorism. A Civil Guard, formed in 1974 by the government to prevent terrorism, consists of volunteers performing neighbourhood-watch and patrol duties.

HEALTH AND WELFARE

The Ministry of Health maintains its own public and preventive health services, including hospitals and clinics, and it supervises the institutions of nongovernmental organizations. A national health insurance program assures hospitalization coverage and basic medical care for all.

Several health maintenance organizations are open to all Israelis, the largest of which, Kupat Holim—with its own physicians, clinics, and hospital—is run by the Histadrut labour union and is recognized worldwide as an exemplary health care organization. Israel ranks highly among the countries in the world in terms of the proportion of its GNP spent on health care and its rates of life expectancy and infant mortality. There are many private, voluntary organizations dealing with first aid, children's health, and care for the aged and those with special needs.

The Ministry of Labour and Social Affairs supervises the service bureaus that deal with family, youth, and community welfare, as well as with rehabilitation of the handicapped. Most of these bureaus operate within local or regional government. Membership in the country's social-insurance plan is compulsory. The program provides welfare, child care and family allowances, income maintenance, disability insurance, old-age pensions, and long-term care for the elderly.

EDUCATION

Schooling is obligatory and free for children between the ages of 5 and 15 and free, but not compulsory, for those 16 and 17. Young people between the ages of 14 and 18, however, who have not completed secondary schooling are obliged to attend special classes. Parents may choose to send children to state secular schools, state religious schools, or private religious schools. For Arab students, there is a system of schools in which Arabic is the primary language of instruction. The school syllabus is supplemented by radio and television educational programming in both Hebrew and Arabic. The educational system gives special attention to agricultural and technical training. Adult education for immigrants assists in their cultural integration.

Hebrew University of Jerusalem

The Hebrew University of Jerusalem is a state-subsidized institution of higher learning in Jerusalem. Israel's foremost university, it attracts many Jewish students from abroad. Originally inaugurated (1925) on Mount Scopus, it was transferred to Giv'at Ram in the Israeli-controlled sector of Jerusalem after 1948, when Mount Scopus became a demilitarized Israeli area within Jordanian territory. After the Israeli reoccupation of Mount Scopus in 1967, the university used both campuses, and Arab students began attending. It has faculties of humanities, science, social sciences, law, agriculture, dental medicine, and medicine, and schools of education, social work, pharmacy, home economics, and applied science and technology and a graduate library school.

In addition to the Hebrew University of Jerusalem (1925), the Technion-Israel Institute of Technology in Haifa (1924), and the Weizmann Institute of Science in Reḥovot (1934), a number of institutions of higher learning have been founded since 1948, including the universities of Tel Aviv and Haifa, Bar-Ilan University (religious, located near Tel Aviv), Ben-Gurion University of the Negev in Beersheba, and the Open University of Israel (formerly Everyman's University) in Tel Aviv. The language of instruction at Israeli universities is Hebrew, while the teaching system represents a mixture of European and American methods. In the 1990s a number of regional community colleges were established, and several foreign universities began offering specialized professional degrees in fields such as law, business, and education. Academic freedom in the universities is protected by Israeli law.

ISRAELI CULTURAL LIFE

There has been little cultural interchange between the Jewish and Arab sections of Israel's population, although Jews arriving in Israel from communities throughout the world, including the Arab-Muslim Middle East, have brought with them both their own cultural inheritance and elements absorbed from the majority cultures in which they dwelt over the centuries.

The intermingling of the Ashkenazi, Sephardi, and Middle Eastern traditions has been of profound importance in forging modern Israel. However, the arrival of immigrants from Russia and other former Soviet republics has slowed the trend, common among immigrants from central Europe and America, toward creating a cultural synthesis embracing East, West, and native Israeli society. The revival of the Hebrew language, not spoken since biblical times, has also been of great importance in the development of Israel's modern culture. This diverse cultural heritage and shared language, along with a common Jewish tradition, both religious and historical, form the foundation of cultural life in Israel.

THE ARTS

The Israel Philharmonic Orchestra has earned a worldwide reputation for classical music, and Israeli artists such as violinists Itzhak Perlman and Pinchas Zukerman and pianist and conductor Daniel Barenboim have had prominent international careers. Folk dancing and popular singing enjoy widespread interest and combine foreign elements with original creative manifestations. The Sephardic, Ashkenazic, and Arab Palestinian communities have all preserved parts of their ethnic music and dance traditions.

CHAPTER 6

S. Y. Agnon

(b. July 17, 1888, Buczacz, Galicia, Austria-Hungary [now Buchach, Ukraine]—d. Feb. 17, 1970, Reḥovot, Israel)

S.Y. Agnon, the pseudonym of Shmuel Yosef Halevi Czaczkes, was an Israeli writer who was one of the leading modern Hebrew novelists and short-story writers. In 1966 he was the corecipient, with Nelly Sachs, of the Nobel Prize for Literature.

Born of a family of Polish Jewish merchants, rabbis, and scholars, Agnon wrote at first (1903–06) in Yiddish and Hebrew, under his own name and various pseudonyms. Soon after settling in Palestine in 1907, however, he took the surname Agnon and chose Hebrew as the language in which to unfold his dramatic, visionary, highly polished narratives.

Agnon's real literary debut was made with *Agunot* (1908; "Forsaken Wives"), his first "Palestinian" story. His first major work was the novel *Hakhnasat kalah,* 2 vol. (1919; *The Bridal Canopy*). Its hero, Reb Yudel Hasid, is the embodiment of every wandering, drifting Jew in the ghettos of the tsarist and Austro-Hungarian empires. His second novel, *Oreaḥ nata la-lun* (1938; *A Guest for the Night*), describes the material and moral decay of European Jewry after World War I. His third and perhaps greatest novel, *Temol shilshom* (1945;."The Day Before Yesterday"), examines the problems facing the westernized Jew who immigrates to Israel. This is neither a realistic story (like some of the early tales) nor a symbolic autobiography, yet it can be understood only in the light of Agnon's own actual and spiritual experience.

All Agnon's works are the final result of innumerable Proust-like revisions, as is shown by the many manuscripts in existence and by the variety of the printed texts. Already there are two widely different versions of his collected works, one in 11 volumes (*Kol sipurav shel Shmuel Yosef Agnon*, vol. 1–6, Berlin, 1931–35; 7–11, Jerusalem and Tel Aviv, 1939–52) and one in 8 volumes (Tel Aviv, 1953–62). The archaic structure of his prose presents great difficulties for the translator, yet even in translation his power is unmistakable.

Agnon edited an anthology of folktales inspired by the High Holidays of the Jewish year, *Yamim nora'im* (1938; *Days of Awe*, 1948), and a selection of famous rabbinic texts, *Sefer, sofer, ve-sipur* (1938). An autobiographical sketch appeared in 1958. Translations of his works include *In the Heart of the Seas* (1948; *Bi-levav yamim*) and *Two Tales* (1966; *Edo ve-enam*).

In 2000 the Education Ministry began including Israeli-Arab writers in the literature curriculum of state secular schools. Painting and sculpture are still largely influenced by European schools, but local styles have begun to emerge, and several "primitive" artists whose works depict biblical and local themes have become popular. In literature, poetry, and drama, a concentration on themes of the Diaspora is giving way to an interest in national themes, including the Holocaust. Among Israel's most distinguished writers is S.Y. Agnon (1888–1970), who received the Nobel Prize for Literature in 1966.

Thanks to an advanced and pervasive communication infrastructure, including cable, satellite, and Internet access, Israeli popular culture is well informed and tuned to the latest international trends and performers. New Israeli pop singers and groups performing in Hebrew emerge frequently. The sound is global and is influenced by folk, rock, and all the latest pop styles, but the lyrics are uniquely Israeli, reflecting the concerns of the country's youth. At the same time lively and locally produced talk shows in Hebrew are prime-time favourites. In addition to cable and satellite access, Arab neighbourhoods and towns bristle with TV antennas permitting reception from neighbouring Arab countries and making Arabic pop music widely available.

Itzhak Perlman

(b. Aug. 31, 1945, Tel Aviv, Palestine [now Tel Aviv–Yafo, Israel])

Itzhak Perlman is an Israeli-American violinist known for his brilliant virtuoso technique. His refinement of detail led many to regard him as one of the finest performers of the major violin repertoire of his time.

Perlman contracted polio at age four, which left his legs paralyzed. His first public concert was in Tel Aviv when he was 10. In 1958 he went to the United States to study at the Juilliard School in New York City with the renowned teachers Ivan Galamian and Dorothy DeLay; in that same year he performed before a national television audience on the *Ed Sullivan Show*. He made his Carnegie Hall (New York City) debut in 1963 and won the prestigious Leventritt Prize a year later, which brought him immediate engagements with major American orchestras. (The Leventritt Foundation awarded its violin

and piano prizes only sporadically; the rarity of the prize and the value of the guaranteed engagements that came with it separated the Leventritt from other competitions.) As well as performing virtually the entire classical concert repertoire, he occasionally played with klezmer (traditional Jewish dance music) and jazz groups. He also played the solo violin passages in John Williams's Oscar-winning score for the movie *Schindler's List* (1993).

As a conductor he worked with many of the great orchestras. He held the position of

Israeli-American violinist Itzhak Perlman. Donald Kravitz/Getty Images principal guest conductor with the Detroit Symphony from 2001 to 2005 and was music adviser of the St. Louis (Mo.) Symphony from 2002 to 2004. Perlman was also a teacher, regularly giving violin master classes and cofounding in 1998 (with his wife, Toby) the Perlman Music Program to encourage gifted string players aged 12 to 18. In addition to 15 Grammy Awards received between 1977 and 1995, Perlman was a recipient of the U.S. Medal of Freedom (1986), the National Medal of Arts (2000), and a Kennedy Center Honor (2003).

CULTURAL INSTITUTIONS

Israel has a rich and varied range of cultural institutions, including major libraries, an art institute and artists' colonies, art museums, institutes for archeology and folk life, theatres, concert halls and performing arts centres, and movie houses. A thriving film industry has emerged. In 1953 the Israeli government established the Academy of the Hebrew Language as the supreme authority on all questions related to the language and its usages, and it founded the Israel Academy of Sciences and Humanities in 1959. The Jewish National and University Library in Jerusalem is preeminent among the country's several hundred libraries. Habima, Israel's national theatre, was founded in Moscow in 1917 and moved to Palestine in 1931. There are a number of other theatres in the country, some of them in the kibbutzim. Foremost among the many art galleries and museums is the Israel Museum in Jerusalem, which also houses part of the archaeological collection of the government's Department of Antiquities. The discovery of the Dead Sea Scrolls in 1947 was a powerful stimulus to biblical and historical research in the country.

SPORTS AND RECREATION

A wide variety of sports are pursued in Israel, from organized team sports such as football (soccer) and basketball—two perennial favourites—to popular outdoor pastimes such as mountain biking, windsurfing, and scuba diving.

Jewish pioneers formed the Palestine Olympic Committee in 1933, but the first Israeli team did not participate in the games until the 1952 Summer Games at Helsinki, Finland. However, Israel's Olympic team is perhaps best remembered for the tragic kidnapping and murder of 11 of its members by Palestinian militants at the 1972 Summer Games in Munich, West Germany.

Israel is the home of the Maccabiah Games, an international gathering of Jewish athletes competing in a wide variety of athletic contests and sports that range from traditional Olympic-style events such as track and field and swimming to team and individual pursuits such as squash, bridge, table tennis, and baseball. Established in 1932 by the World Maccabi Union, a Jewish sports foundation, the games

The 1972 Olympic Games were disrupted when a small group of Palestinian militants—one of whom is seen here—kidnapped Israeli athletes. Getty Images

are held every four years and draw thousands of competitors. Beyond being an important athletic competition, the Maccabiah Games are a major cultural event in the world Jewish community.

MEDIA AND PUBLISHING

Tel Aviv is the centre of newspaper publishing in Israel. In the past newspapers were often associated with a political party, but most have now passed to private ownership. Most newspapers are written in Hebrew, but a considerable number are also published in Yiddish, English, German, Arabic, Russian, Polish, French, Bulgarian, and Romanian. There are hundreds of other periodicals, of which more than half are in Hebrew.

The Israel Broadcasting Authority, whose members are appointed by the president, controls and licenses the broadcasting industry. Commercial radio and broadcasting has been allowed since 1986. There are two public radio networks—one providing classical programming and the other more popular music—and an armed forces station; in addition several private radio stations have been established since 1986. Programs are broadcast mainly in Hebrew, Arabic, and English but also in a wide variety of other languages, including Yiddish, Russian, Ladino (a Spanish dialect of the Sephardic Jews), and Moghrabi (Moroccan Judeo-Arabic).

Television programming, introduced in 1966, is in Hebrew and Arabic. There are two television networks, one of which is government-owned and the other privately funded, and an educational television service. Cable and direct-dish television are available in much of the country, providing a wide range of international programming via satellite, and Internet access is widely available.

CHAPTER 7

ISRAEL: PAST AND PRESENT

Israel is the world's first Jewish state in two millennia. It represents for Jews the restoration of their homeland after the centuries-long Diaspora that followed the demise of the Herodian kingdom in the 1st century CE. As such, it remains the focus of widespread Jewish immigration, and more than one-third of world Jewry now lives there.

The country, little more than six decades old, was born in the midst of war. It took Israel three decades and numerous conflicts, large and small, to achieve its first peace treaty with a neighbouring Arab country, Egypt. That process has been complicated by Israel's relations with the Palestinians, many of whom were displaced by the Arab-Israeli war in 1948 or came under Israeli rule following the Six-Day War in 1967. Only since the signing of the Oslo Accords in 1993 has an inclusive peace settlement with other Arab states and with the region's Palestinian Arabs been a possibility.

Israel's national security policy has been dominated by the prime minister and shaped by coalition politics—often disrupted by social and religious issues—that have characterized the state since its creation. While the country's two major parties, the left-wing Labour and right-wing Likud, often found a consensus on security issues, especially during crises, they retained an important difference that dates to the early years of Zionism. Both parties affirm Jewish rights to the biblical land of Israel (an area only slightly larger than the U.S. state of Vermont), but Labour has been ready, as the price of peace, to cede sovereignty to the Arabs of part of the area it occupied after the 1967 war, while Likud has insisted that control of that territory is vital to Israel's security. Neither political party, however, has been prepared to accept the return to Israel of large numbers of Palestinian refugees. In spite of extensive peace talks following Oslo, and a peace treaty with Jordan (1994) Israel has not been able to come to an amicable peace with Syria or Lebanon or with the Palestinians. Persistent bouts of violence have dimmed hopes for peace.

Domestically, Israel moved steadily from an economy directed by the state to one that was more market oriented. A novel feature of the earlier economy was the kibbutz, a collective settlement movement that exemplified the Labour-Zionist movement's ideals of sacrifice and leadership. After Labour lost political power to the non-socialist Likud opposition in 1977, the kibbutz ideal began to wane and with it the socialist and secular beliefs so strong at Israel's birth. The huge influx of Sephardic Jews in the 1950s and Russian Jews in the 1980s and '90s forced more political, social, and economic changes, as these groups acquired increasing power and influence. A crucial unresolved question remained: the relationship between religion and state.

ORIGINS OF A MODERN JEWISH STATE

Modern Israel springs from both religious and political sources. The biblical promise of a land for the Jews and a return to the Temple in Jerusalem were enshrined in Judaism and sustained Jewish identity through an exile of 19 centuries following the failed revolts in Judaea against the Romans early in the Common Era. By the 1800s, fewer than 25,000 Jews still lived in their ancient homeland, and these were largely concentrated in Jerusalem, then a provincial backwater of the Ottoman Empire.

ZIONISM

In the 1880s, a rise in European anti-Semitism and revived Jewish national pride combined to inspire a new wave of emigration to Palestine in the form of agricultural colonies financed by the Rothschilds and other wealthy families. Political Zionism came a decade later, when the Austrian journalist Theodor Herzl began advocating a Jewish state as the political solution for both anti-Semitism (he had covered the sensational Dreyfus affair in France) and a Jewish secular identity. Herzl's brief and dramatic bid for international support from the major powers at the First Zionist Congress (August 1897) failed, but, after his death in 1904, the surviving Zionist organization under the leadership of Chaim Weizmann undertook a major effort to increase the Jewish population in Palestine while continuing to search for political assistance.

These efforts could only be on a small scale while the Ottoman Turks ruled what the Europeans called Palestine (from Palaestina, "Land of the Philistines," the Latin name given Judaea by the Romans). But in 1917, during World War I, the Zionists persuaded the British government to issue the Balfour Declaration, a document

Theodor Herzl, an Austrian journalist and Zionist who advocated for the establishment of an independent Jewish state partly as a means to combat anti-Semitism. Imagno/Hulton Archive/Getty Images

that committed Britain to facilitate the establishment of a "national home for the Jewish people" in Palestine. Amid considerable controversy over conflicting wartime promises to the Arabs and French, Britain succeeded in gaining the endorsement of the declaration by the new League of Nations, which placed Palestine under British mandate. This achievement reflected a heady mixture of religious and imperial motivations that Britain would find difficult to reconcile in the troubled years ahead.

Balfour Declaration

The Balfour Declaration (Nov. 2, 1917) was a statement of British support for "the establishment in Palestine of a national home for the Jewish people." It was made in a letter from Arthur James Balfour, the British foreign secretary, to Lionel Walter Rothschild, 2nd Baron Rothschild (of Tring), a leader of British Jewry. Though the precise meaning of the correspondence has been disputed, its statements were generally contradictory to both the Sykes-Picot Agreement (a secret convention between Britain and France) and the Ḥusayn-McMahon correspondence (an exchange of letters between the British high commissioner in Egypt, Sir Henry McMahon, and Ḥusayn ibn ʿAlī, then emir of Mecca), which in turn contradicted one another.

The Balfour Declaration, issued through the continued efforts of Chaim Weizmann and Nahum Sokolow, Zionist leaders in London, fell short of the expectations of the Zionists, who had asked for the reconstitution of Palestine as "the" Jewish national home. The declaration specifically stipulated that "nothing shall be done which may prejudice the civil and religious rights of existing non-Jewish communities in Palestine." The document, however, said nothing of the political or national rights of these communities and did not refer to them by name. Nevertheless, the declaration aroused enthusiastic hopes among Zionists and seemed the fulfillment of the aims of the World Zionist Organization.

The British government hoped that the declaration would rally Jewish opinion, especially in the United States, to the side of the Allied powers against the Central Powers during World War I

(1914–18). They hoped also that the settlement in Palestine of a pro-British Jewish population might help to protect the approaches to the Suez Canal in neighbouring Egypt and thus ensure a vital communication route to British colonial possessions in India.

The Balfour Declaration was endorsed by the principal Allied powers and was included in the British mandate over Palestine, formally approved by the newly created League of Nations on July 24, 1922. In May 1939 the British government altered its policy in a White Paper recommending a limit of 75,000 further immigrants and an end to immigration by 1944, unless the Arabs consented to further immigration. Zionists condemned the new policy, accusing Britain of favouring the resident Palestinian Arabs of the region. This point was made moot by the outbreak of World War II (1939–45) and the founding of the State of Israel in 1948.

IMMIGRATION AND CONFLICT

The Zionist goal of Jewish statehood was violently opposed by the local Arab leaders, who saw the Ottoman defeat as an opportunity either to create their own state or to join a larger Arab entity—thus reviving the old Arab empire of early Islamic times. British efforts to bring the Zionists and the Arabs together in a cooperative government failed, and serious disorders, escalating into organized violence, were to mark the mandate, culminating in the Arab Revolt of 1936–39. This period also marked the birth of local Jewish defense forces. The largest and most widely representative of the various militias, the Haganah ("Defense") was a branch of the Jewish Agency, the organization most responsible for bringing Jews to Israel.

The most effective of the main, pre-state militias were associated with political factions from both the right and left wings of Zionist politics. The Irgun Zvai Leumi and its even more violent splinter group, Lehi (also known as the Stern Gang), were affiliated with the ultraconservative

Revisionist Party, founded by Vladimir Zev Jabotinsky. (The Revisionists withdrew from the main Zionist institutions in 1935 in protest against Jewish cooperation with the British mandate.) Another group, the Palmach, though technically an elite arm of the Haganah, was heavily influenced by a Marxist-socialist party, Achdut HaAvoda, and recruited many of its members from socialist-oriented kibbutzim. Members of these militias were to play an important role in Israeli politics for the next half century; Yigal Allon, Moshe Dayan, and Yitzhak Rabin were high-ranking members of the Haganah-Palmach, Menachem Begin led the Irgun, and Yitzhak Shamir was a prominent member of the Lehi. Three of these men—Rabin, Shamir, and Begin—would later become prime ministers of Israel.

Britain encouraged Jewish immigration in the 1920s, but the onset of the worldwide Great Depression of the 1930s and the flight of refugees from Nazi Germany led to a change in policy. The British government proposed the partition of Palestine into mutually dependent Arab and Jewish states. When this was rejected by the Arabs, London decided in 1939 to restrict Jewish immigration severely in the hope that it would retain Arab support against Germany and Italy. Palestine was thus largely closed off to Jews fleeing Nazi-dominated Europe during World War II. In spite of this fact, the majority of the Jewish population supported the Allies during the war while seeking, when possible, clandestine Jewish immigration to Palestine. The Jewish community, which was less than 100,000 in 1919, numbered some 600,000 by the end of the war. The Arabs of Palestine had also increased under the mandate (through high birth rates and immigration) from about 440,000 to roughly one million in 1940.

The pre-Holocaust Zionist struggle to secure international support, overcome Arab opposition, and promote immigration resumed with special fervour after 1945, when the true extent of Jewish losses in Europe became evident. In Britain, the newly elected government of Prime Minister Clement Attlee, alarmed by growing violence in Palestine between Arabs and Jewish immigrants, decided to end the mandate, but it was unable to do so in a peaceful way. Attlee and his foreign secretary, Ernest Bevin, came under pressure by the Zionists and their sympathizers, especially Pres. Harry S. Truman in the United States, to admit the desperate remnant of European Jewry into Palestine; they were equally pressured by local and regional Arab opponents of a Jewish state to put an end to further immigration. Both sides, Arab and Jewish, violently assailed the reinforced garrison in Palestine of the war-weakened British.

Finally, London turned the problem over to the newly formed UN, and on Nov. 29, 1947, the UN General Assembly voted to divide British-ruled Palestine into two states, one Jewish and the other Arab. The Zionists favoured the proposal: it recognized a Jewish state and allotted a substantial portion of Palestine west of the Jordan River to it. As almost half of the population of the Jewish state would be Arab, however, this decision was immediately opposed by the Arabs who, under the ostensible leadership of Hajj Amīn al-Ḥusaynī, the grand mufti of Jerusalem, attacked Jews throughout Palestine as the British withdrew. The fighting was savage, and many civilians were slain: incidents cited include the killing of 250 Arab villagers by a group of Irgun commandos in the village of Dayr Yāsīn and the massacre of 77 members of a Hadassah medical convoy by Palestinian Arabs.

THE WAR OF 1948 AND THE ESTABLISHMENT OF ISRAEL

The Zionist militias gained the upper hand over the Palestinians through skill and pluck, aided considerably by intra-Arab rivalries. Israel's declaration of independence on May 14, 1948, was quickly recognized by the United States, the Soviet Union, and many other governments, fulfilling the Zionist dream of an internationally approved Jewish state. Neither the UN nor the world leaders, however, could spare Israel from immediate invasion by the armies of five Arab states—Egypt, Iraq, Lebanon, Syria, and Transjordan (now Jordan)—and within a few days, the state's survival appeared to be at stake.

David Ben-Gurion (standing), *officially proclaims Israel an independent state in May 1948. Ben-Gurion was named the state's first prime minister.* AFP/Getty Images

The Israeli forces, desperately short of arms and training, still had the advantage of having just beaten al-Ḥusaynī's irregulars, and their morale was high. David Ben-Gurion, the new prime minister, had also, soon after independence, unified the military command, although this process was bloody. When an Irgun ship called the *Altalena* attempted to land near Tel Aviv in June 1948 under conditions unacceptable to Ben-Gurion, he ordered it stopped. Troops commanded by Yitzhak Rabin fired on the vessel, killing 82 people (Menachem Begin was one of the survivors). The Irgun and Palmach finally consented to the unified command, but relations between the Labour movement Ben-Gurion had established and its right-wing opposition, founded in Jabotinsky's Revisionist Party, were poisoned for years.

The Arab invaders far outnumbered the Zionists but fielded only a few well-trained units. In addition, some Arab logistical lines were long, making resupply and communication difficult. The most formidable Arab force was Transjordan's British-led Arab Legion, but the Jordanian ruler, King 'Abdullāh, had secret relations with the Zionists and strongly opposed a Palestinian state led by his enemy al-Ḥusaynī. Other states, such as Egypt and Iraq, also had different objectives, and this internal strife, disorganization, and military ineptitude prevented the Arabs from mounting a coordinated attack.

Small numbers of Israeli forces were able to keep Egyptian, Iraqi, and Jordanian units from entering Tel Aviv and cutting off Jerusalem from the rest of the newly founded country during the crucial first month of the war. In June all sides accepted a UN cease-fire, and the nearly exhausted Israelis reequipped themselves, sometimes from secret sources. Notable was the clandestine effort by Soviet-dominated Czechoslovakia, which offered Israel both arms and an airfield — Soviet leader Joseph Stalin had decided that the Jewish state might be a useful thorn in the side of Britain and the United States, his Cold War enemies.

Fierce fighting resumed in early July and continued for months interspersed with brief truces. The Israelis drove back the Egyptian and Iraqi forces that menaced the south and central parts of the coastal plain. However, the old walled city of Jerusalem, containing the Western Wall, the last remnant of the ancient Temple destroyed by the Romans and held holy by Jews, was occupied by the Jordanians, and Jerusalem's lifeline to the coast was jeopardized. The Egyptians held Gaza, and the Syrians entrenched themselves in the Golan Heights overlooking Galilee. The 1948 war was Israel's costliest: more than 6,000 were killed and 30,000 wounded out of a population of only 780,000.

Initial UN mediation conducted by Swedish diplomat Count Folke Bernadotte produced a peace plan rejected by all sides, and Bernadotte himself was murdered by Lehi extremists in September 1948. When Israel secured the final armistice of the war in July 1949, the new state controlled one-fifth more territory than the original partition plan had specified and rejected a return to the original partition line. Jordan occupied the West Bank, which was much of the area assigned by the UN to the stillborn Palestinian state, and, although figures are disputed, it is believed that more than 600,000 (and perhaps more than 700,000) Arab refugees fled their homes in an exodus that had begun even before May 1948. Some were forced out by Israeli troops, notably from the towns of Lod and Ramla in the strategic area near Tel Aviv airport. The Israeli government refused to permit these refugees, who gathered under UN care in camps in Gaza, the West Bank, southern Lebanon, and Syria, to return to their homes inside Israel, and many Palestinians were to stay in these camps indefinitely.

Israel's victory in the war did not bring peace. The Arabs, who were humiliated by defeat and still bitterly divided, refused to recognize the Jewish state. In early

1949, the Arab countries announced a state of war with Israel and organized an economic and political boycott of the country.

THE BEN-GURION ERA

The new Israeli state thus had to deal with challenges similar to those faced by the pre-1948 Zionist movement and needed foreign assistance, an effective strategy to hold off the Arabs, and massive Jewish immigration to settle the land in order to survive. All of this had to be done at once, and none of it could be possible without Israeli national unity.

Israel's first regular election in 1949 returned Ben-Gurion to power but did not give his Mapai (Labour) Party a majority. This set a pattern, and every Israeli government since independence has been formed as a coalition. Ben-Gurion sought a centrist position, condemning those to his left as pro-Soviet and those to his right as antidemocratic. He buttressed these arrangements by adding the Zionist religious parties to his largely secular coalition in what became known as the "status quo." The Orthodox Jewish religious parties backed Ben-Gurion on security issues, while Ben-Gurion supported an Orthodox monopoly over the control of marriage, divorce, conversion, and other personal status issues. Part of the status quo, however, included rejecting the idea of drafting a written constitution or bill of rights, and the Jewish content of the Jewish state thus would be defined by the rough-and-tumble of Israeli politics and the evolution of Israeli society.

EMERGENCE OF A NATION

During the early years, Israel had to absorb a major influx of immigrants, including several hundred thousand nearly destitute Holocaust survivors and a large influx of Sephardic Jews from Arab states, who felt increasingly insecure in their home countries following the Arab defeat in 1948. As a result, the Knesset passed the Law of Return in 1950, granting Jews immediate citizenship. This law, however, proved to be controversial in later years when the question of "who is a Jew?" raised other issues in the Jewish state, including those of the immigration of non-Jewish relatives, religious conversion, and, in light of the Orthodox monopoly over such matters, the issue of who is truly qualified to be a rabbi. Ben-Gurion's coalition was also frequently disturbed by quarrels over education and the role religion was to play in it. Orthodox support for the government often faltered over what they saw to be state interference in a religious domain.

No less serious was the question of ethnicity. The Sephardim, or Oriental Jews, were mostly from urban and traditional societies, and after arriving in Israel they encountered an Ashkenazic, or European, Zionist establishment intent on creating a new Israeli culture and settling these predominantly urban newcomers in rural and isolated villages and development towns. The Sephardim soon grew to resent what they regarded as a patronizing Ashkenazic elite, and eventually this was to hurt Labour at the ballot box.

Israel was impoverished, and its economy emerged from severe austerity only after 1952 when the country began to obtain substantial international aid, including grants from Jewish charities, revenue from the sale of bonds, and U.S. government assistance. Beginning in 1953, Ben-Gurion secured economic aid from what was then West Germany, a highly controversial act that was seen by many as reparations for the Holocaust. This action brought about violent protests led by members of Menachem

Begin's Ḥerut Party (the successor to the Revisionists), who felt that any such aid would be an abomination.

CONTINUING TENSIONS

In spite of its victory in the 1948 war, Israel soon faced new and severe threats. Arab refugees infiltrated the armistice lines seeking to reclaim fields and houses. Soon, irregular Arab forces, drawn from refugee camps outside Israel's borders, began to attack Israeli villages, farms, and road traffic. Israel also contained a sizable minority of Arabs (then roughly one-sixth of the population), who were kept under military rule in certain areas until 1966 and, in some cases, were relocated away from border zones.

The Israelis intensively cultivated the land on their side of the border, while the Arabs tended to leave their side barren—hence the phrase "green line," referring to the border between the two sides. The green lines themselves were difficult to defend; only 12 miles (19 km) separated Jordanian army positions from the Mediterranean, and the road connecting Jerusalem with the rest of the Israel was within rifle range of Arab sharpshooters. Israel's potential allies, including the United States, were preoccupied with the Cold War and were willing to placate Arab leaders in order to limit Soviet influence among the Arab states, especially Egypt, which looked to Moscow for help against Britain and France, the remaining colonial powers in the region.

Israel's best chance for peace was King 'Abdullāh of Jordan, but in 1950 Palestinian and Arab opposition forced him to abandon a secretly negotiated nonbelligerency agreement. When the Egyptians tried unsuccessfully to establish a rump Palestinian state in Gaza under al-Ḥusaynī, 'Abdullāh announced the annexation of the West Bank, which his country had occupied two years earlier. Then, in July 1951, the Jordanian king was assassinated on the Temple Mount in Jerusalem by a Palestinian. His grandson, the future King Ḥussein, barely escaped injury and was to continue ʿAbdullāh's policy of clandestine contact with Israel but, like his grandfather, never felt politically strong enough to make a separate peace.

In the period 1949–53 Arab attacks killed hundreds of Israelis, four-fifths of whom were civilian. In early 1953 Israel decided to take the offensive against Arab guerrillas who were infiltrating from Jordan and the Egyptian-run Gaza Strip. The Israel Defense Forces (IDF) escalated retaliations, fighting pitched battles not only with guerrillas but with regular Jordanian and Egyptian army units. The Israelis also launched undercover operations, one of which, the so-called Lavon affair, was a botched attempt by Israeli intelligence to hurt Egypt's reputation in the United States by staging attacks on U.S. facilities in Egypt and blaming Arab extremists.

THE SUEZ CRISIS

The Israeli raids humiliated Egypt's nationalist government headed by Gamal Abdel Nasser, a veteran of the 1948 war and leader of the group that had overthrown King Farouk in 1952. Nasser sought to lead the Arabs in expelling British and French imperial influence and regarded Israel as a symbol of foreign aggression. After he failed to obtain American arms to repel the Israeli attacks, Nasser trumped both Israel and his Western adversaries when in October 1955 he signed a security agreement with the Soviet Union and a major arms deal with Czechoslovakia that threatened overnight to erase Israel's tenuous margin of military superiority, especially in aircraft. He also announced a blockade of the Strait of Tiran, the outlet of Israel's southern port city of Elat.

Ben-Gurion, exhausted by political struggles, had left the premiership in late 1953 to Moshe Sharett, who hoped that vigorous international diplomacy might relieve Israel's insecurity. It did not. Ben-Gurion had a different approach, and returning as prime minister in late 1955 after the Czech-Egyptian arms deal, he soon began to plan a preemptive attack against Egypt before that country's new weaponry gave it strategic superiority. The preparations for an Israeli attack coincided with the Anglo-French decision to regain the Suez Canal, which Nasser had nationalized in July 1956 in spite of agreements putting it under international control. The French brokered a secret alliance with Israel and Britain, and in October IDF troops, under the leadership of Moshe Dayan, swiftly broke the Egyptian lines in the Sinai. The Israeli attack provided the cover for a ruse in which the British and French invaded the canal zone under the pretext of protecting it. This duplicity infuriated American Pres. Dwight D. Eisenhower, who compelled the British and French governments to withdraw their troops, effectively ending much of the influence of those two countries in the region. Israel was also compelled to return to the old armistice lines, but not before the United States had agreed to placing a UN peacekeeping force in the Sinai. American Secretary of State John Foster Dulles also promised in writing that the United States would treat the Strait of Tiran as an international waterway and keep it open.

These arrangements did not lead to peace negotiations, but they did impose a calm over Israel's southern border for nearly a decade. A regional arms race began in the absence of any movement toward peace, and Shimon Peres, Ben-Gurion's deputy defense minister, found France to be a willing supplier. The French-designed nuclear reactor in Dimona was widely suspected of being the kernel of an Israeli nuclear weapons program, while French Mirage jets became the backbone of Israel's air force. The Israelis also obtained a large indirect supply of arms from the United States, with West Germany as the intermediary. Israel, under the leadership of IDF Chief of Staff Yitzhak Rabin, turned its military into a highly professional organization.

LABOUR RULE AFTER BEN-GURION

Ben-Gurion stepped down as prime minister in June 1963, angered by the results of a review of the decade-old Lavon affair that had not, in his view, attached blame adequately to those responsible for that failed and illegal operation. His efforts at building the Israeli state had also brought him into conflict with his own party's ideology, the Orthodox religious establishment, and the international Zionist movement. Gathering about him a group of younger leaders in 1965, notably Shimon Peres and Moshe Dayan, Ben-Gurion organized a new political party, Rafi, though he eventually retired from politics permanently in 1970 when that party failed to generate support.

THE SIX-DAY WAR

Ben-Gurion's successor, Levi Eshkol, had much less experience in defense issues and relied heavily on Rabin. Neither the Jordanian nor the Syrian borders were quiet during the years leading up to the Six-Day War, but all Israelis were taken by surprise when in May 1967 increasingly violent clashes with Palestinian guerrillas and Syrian army forces along Lake Tiberias led to a general crisis. The Soviet Union alleged that Israel was mobilizing to attack Syria, and the Syrian government, in turn, chided President Nasser of Egypt for inaction. Nasser then mobilized his own forces,

which he promptly sent into the Sinai after he ordered that
UN forces there be withdrawn, and announced a blockade of the Strait of Tiran. The encirclement of Israel was
complete when King Hussein of Jordan, in spite of secret
Israeli pleas, felt compelled to join the Arab war coalition.

In reaction, Eshkol mobilized the IDF and sent
his foreign minister, Abba Eban, on a futile trip to seek
French, British, and American aid. After Rabin suffered a
breakdown from exhaustion, the coalition parties forced
Eshkol to appoint Moshe Dayan as defense minister
and to create a national unity government that included
Menachem Begin, the main opposition leader. The next
day, June 5, Israeli planes destroyed the Egyptian air force
on the ground in a preemptive strike that began the total
rout of all Egyptian, Jordanian, and Syrian forces. Israeli
troops captured huge quantities of arms and took many
prisoners. Six days later, Israeli troops stood victorious
along the Suez Canal, on the banks of the Jordan River, and
atop the Golan Heights. Most significant to all involved,
Israel had captured the remaining sections of Jerusalem
not already under its control, including the Old City and
the Western Wall.

TROUBLED VICTORY

Israel's triumph in the Six-Day War brought new
territories—the Sinai Peninsula, the West Bank, the
Gaza Strip, the Golan Heights, and East Jerusalem—
under Jewish control. However, the war also brought new
complications, including rule over more than one million additional Palestinians in the occupied territories;
extended military lines along the Suez Canal, the Golan
Heights, and the Jordan River that severely strained its
small standing army; and strong international opposition to the expansion of Israeli control, especially the

absorption of the Old City of Jerusalem. Protesting Israel's surprise attack, French Pres. Charles de Gaulle imposed an arms embargo on Israel, depriving the air force of its only source for advanced warplanes. This situation was resolved when the United States agreed to supply Israel with U.S. fighters to replace the French planes.

It was not clear how military victory could be turned into peace. Shortly after the war's end, Israel began that quest, but it would take more than a decade and involve yet another war before yielding any results. Eshkol's secret offer to trade much of the newly won territory for peace agreements with Egypt, Jordan, and Syria was rejected by Nasser, who, supported by an emergency resupply of Soviet arms, led the Arabs at the Khartoum Arab Summit in the Sudan in August 1967 in a refusal to negotiate directly with Israel. The UN Security Council responded by passing Resolution 242 in November, demanding that Israel withdraw from "occupied territories" and that all parties in the dispute recognize the right of residents of each state to live within "secure and recognized borders." The wording of this statement became crucial to peace negotiations for years to come. By not stating "all the occupied territories" in the English version—the only one accepted by Israel— the resolution left room for the Israelis to negotiate. The Palestinians, the residents of these territories, were mentioned only as refugees, it being presumed that Jordan would represent them.

Nearly two years of fruitless mediation ensued while Israel held the occupied territories with a minimum of force, relied on its air power to deter Arab attack, and—adhering to Dayan's light-handed occupation policy—disturbed the Palestinian population under military rule as little as possible. The Israelis left the Temple Mount in Jerusalem, the local Arab institutions, and indeed the Jordanian legal code throughout the West Bank in the hands of the Palestinians, just as they left Egyptian regulations in place in Gaza.

The Israeli and Palestinian economies were to develop strong links over the next decades, as the underemployed Arab workforce in the occupied territories gravitated to Israeli industries that were chronically short of unskilled labour. Eventually more than 150,000 workers would make the daily commute to Israel, returning to the West Bank and Gaza at night. While the export of Israeli goods to the occupied territories became lucrative, it formed but a small part of the economic exchange between the two sides.

Meanwhile, the Israeli government moved to reclaim areas in the newly occupied territories that had been settled by Jews before 1948, including the Etzion Bloc, an Israeli community on the approach to Jerusalem that had been lost to Jordan after heavy fighting during Israel's war of independence. After the Arabs rejected a quick peace, Yigal Allon, a leading Labour politician and a hero of the 1948 war, devised a plan to settle Jews in strategic areas of the West Bank, Gaza, Sinai, and the Golan Heights. Israel also enlarged the municipal boundaries of Jerusalem and developed new neighbourhoods in order to establish a Jewish majority in the capital; and in the Old City, the government reconstructed the historic Jewish quarter. However, except for East Jerusalem, where the Jewish population increased dramatically in the years of Labour dominance, by 1977 only about 5,000 Israelis lived in these so-called strategic settlements. Other Israelis, guided by the prominent Rabbi Zvi Yehuda Kook, believed that settlement everywhere in the biblical land of Israel would hasten the messianic era. Israelis of this mind established the Gush Emunim ("Bloc of Believers") organization in the West Bank city of Hebron in 1968.

United Nations Resolution 242

UN Resolution 242 was passed in an effort to secure a just and lasting peace in the wake of the Six-Day (June) War of 1967. The Israelis supported the resolution because it called on the Arab states to accept Israel's right "to live in peace within secure and recognized boundaries free from threats or acts of force." Each of the Arab states eventually accepted it (Egypt and Jordan accepted the resolution from the outset) because of its clause calling for Israel to withdraw from the territories conquered in 1967. The PLO rejected it until 1988 because it lacked explicit references to Palestinians. Though never fully implemented, it was the basis of diplomatic efforts to end Arab-Israeli conflicts until the Camp David Accords and remains an important touchstone in any negotiated resolution to the Arab-Israeli conflict.

THE WAR OF ATTRITION

In early 1969 Egypt began what became known as the War of Attrition against Israel. Using heavy artillery, new MiG aircraft, Soviet advisers, and an advanced Soviet-designed surface-to-air missile system, the Egyptians inflicted heavy losses on the Israelis. Golda Meir, who became Israel's prime minister following Eshkol's sudden death in February 1969, escalated the war by ordering massive air raids deep into Egypt. These raids were suspended, however, after the Soviet pilots began to fly combat patrols over parts of Egypt, and the battle shifted to the canal zone. Israel was also beset by guerrilla raids from Jordan, launched by Yāsir 'Arafāt's PLO. These attacks were often on nonmilitary targets, and Israel soon stamped the PLO as a terrorist organization and refused to negotiate with it.

U.S. Pres. Richard Nixon feared an eventual Israeli confrontation with the Soviets and sent Secretary of State William Rogers to intervene with a complex cease-fire proposal, which was accepted by Israel, Egypt, and Jordan in August 1970. This plan specified limits on the deployment of missiles and revived a year-old diplomatic initiative (the Rogers Plan) that insisted on an exchange of territory for peace on all fronts.

Israeli Prime Minister Golda Meir meets with U.S. Pres. Richard Nixon on the lawn of the White House in 1969. Arnold Sachs/Archive Photos/ Getty Images

The Egyptians and Soviets soon violated the agreement by moving their missiles closer to the canal. In Jordan, Hussein's acceptance of the cease-fire ignited savage fighting between the Jordanian army and several PLO militia groups. As the battles intensified, Syria sent tanks to aid the Palestinians, but coordinated Israeli, American, and Jordanian military moves defeated the Syrians and expelled the PLO, whose forces sought refuge in Lebanon.

Meir's gamble had succeeded. Israel's willingness to risk confrontation, even with Soviet pilots along the canal, had strengthened relations with the United States. Hussein's recovery of control in Jordan demoralized Palestinian resistance while securing Israel's eastern border. When Nasser died in September 1970, his successor, Anwar el-Sādāt, did not renew the fighting, seeking instead a partial Israeli pullback from the Suez Canal. Israel eventually rejected this idea, but the crisis had passed.

THE YOM KIPPUR WAR AND THE DECLINE OF LABOUR DOMINANCE

On Oct. 6, 1973—the Jewish Day of Atonement, Yom Kippur—Egyptian and Syrian forces staged a surprise attack on Israeli forces situated on the Suez Canal and the Golan Heights. Israeli confidence in its early warning systems and air superiority was misplaced, and Egyptian missiles were soon taking a heavy toll of Israeli warplanes. The intensity of the Egyptian and Syrian assault, so unlike the situation in 1967, rapidly began to exhaust Israel's reserve stocks of munitions.

With Israel threatened by catastrophe, Prime Minister Meir turned to the United States for aid, while the Israeli general staff hastily improvised a battle strategy. Washington's reluctance to help Israel changed rapidly when the Soviet Union launched its own resupply effort to Egypt and Syria. President Nixon countered by establishing an emergency supply line to Israel, even though the Arab countries imposed a costly oil embargo, and various American allies refused to facilitate the arms shipments.

With reinforcements on the way, the IDF rapidly turned the tide. A daring Israeli helicopter assault disabled portions of the Egyptian air defenses, which allowed Israeli forces commanded by Gen. Ariel Sharon to cross the Suez Canal and threaten to destroy the Egyptian Third Army. On the Golan, Israeli troops, at heavy cost, repulsed the Syrians and advanced to the edge of the Golan plateau on the road to Damascus. At this point, the United States, alarmed by Soviet threats of direct military intervention and on nuclear alert, secured a cease-fire in place.

POLITICAL AND SOCIAL REPERCUSSIONS OF THE WAR

Sādāt persuaded U.S. Secretary of State Henry Kissinger that his country was ready to abandon both its Soviet and Syrian allies for a fresh start with the United States; only Washington, in Sādāt's view, could effectively influence Israel to return the Sinai without further bloodshed. Kissinger, supported by Nixon, successfully pressured Israel to end the war short of a complete Egyptian military defeat and then, through intensive travel between the various capitals—what soon was being called shuttle diplomacy—achieved disengagement agreements on both the Egyptian and Syrian fronts during 1974. This became known as the "step-by-step" process, which was intended to fulfill the intent of Security Council Resolution 242 that territory be exchanged for peace.

Golda Meir's government resigned in April 1974, exhausted and discredited by the war. Still, the Labour Party won a narrow election victory in June by selecting Yitzhak Rabin, hero of the 1967 war and former Israeli ambassador to Washington, to lead its list. The first native-born Israeli to become prime minister, Rabin predicted a period of "seven lean years" until the West, including the United States, would end its heavy dependence on Arab oil. He argued that Israel therefore needed to trade space for time, to coordinate closely with Washington, and to encourage Egypt's new pro-American policy.

Rabin reached a second disengagement agreement with Egypt in September 1975, but little progress was made with Syria. On what had been the "quiet" front—the

West Bank and Gaza—the Labour government's pre-
ferred strategy of negotiations with the more amenable
King Hussein of Jordan (the so-called "Jordanian option")
was threatened in October 1974, when an Arab summit
conference in Rabat, Morocco, declared 'Arafāt's PLO to
be the sole representative of the Palestinians. A year later,
Rabin obtained secret assurances from Kissinger that the
United States would not recognize the PLO as an entity
representing the Palestinians unless that organization
first ceased terrorism and recognized Israel's right to exist.

Meanwhile, the Gush Emunim movement on the
West Bank gathered force after the Yom Kippur War and
between 1974 and 1987 planted small communities near
large Arab populations, greatly complicating Israeli policy
and arousing international opposition. The secular Israeli
government opposed such efforts but rarely used force to
dislodge the settlers, who invoked Zionist rights to the
homeland in their defense. Still, they numbered fewer
than 4,000 when the opposition Likud government of
Menachem Begin came to power in 1977.

DIPLOMATIC IMPASSE

The Yom Kippur War left the country in bad economic
shape. An accelerating rate of inflation just before the
conflict was suddenly combined with a stagnant economy;
prices continued to rise even as demand and production
fell. The international recession reduced demand for
Israeli exports, and, for the first time in years, unemployment became a problem. On top of this, Israel became
heavily indebted by arms purchases—partially offset by
U.S. aid—and the country's international status suffered.
One by one, most of Israel's carefully cultivated African
friends broke relations under the threat of Arab oil sanctions, leaving the Jewish state alone with an equally

isolated South Africa. Further complicating the situation for Israel, the UN General Assembly passed Resolution 3379 in 1975, which equated Zionism with racism, and the PLO gained increasing European and Asian support.

Meanwhile, Rabin was losing political ground at home, harmed by infighting and corruption. Even the remarkable success of Israel's July 1976 raid at the Entebbe, Uganda, airport—in which commandos rescued the Israeli passengers of an Air France plane hijacked by German and Palestinian militants—was of little help. The former general, new to politics, found it difficult to dominate a cabinet in which his chief rival, Shimon Peres, was defense minister, and few others owed him any political allegiance.

A further blow to Rabin fell when he visited Washington in March 1977 to meet with the new American president, Jimmy Carter, who advocated a "comprehensive approach" to Middle East peace instead of the Kissinger step-by-step plan. Carter sought an international conference to resolve all the major issues between Israel and the Arabs and advocated a "homeland" for the Palestinians. For Israelis, this notion (and its similarity to the wording of the Balfour Declaration) was a code word for a Palestinian state, and they hotly opposed it—not least because it also implied a leadership role for the PLO. Rabin, facing a major quarrel with the United States and beset by a personal scandal—his wife had maintained an illegal bank account in Washington from his days as ambassador—resigned in April, and Shimon Peres became Labour's new party leader.

ISRAEL UNDER LIKUD

To general surprise, the Likud Party, led by Menachem Begin, won the May 1977 election, inaugurating the first non-Labour-led government in Israel's history. Begin's

campaign benefited immensely from Sephardic resentment over the patronizing attitude of the Labour
establishment and its treatment of non-European Jewish
immigrants as second-class citizens. The Sephardim supported Likud in large numbers. In addition, a new "clean
government" party drew votes from Labour, and its leader,
Yigael Yadin, an eminent archaeologist and a hero of the
1948 war, joined the cabinet. Also included in Begin's cabinet were Ezer Weizman, an air force commander in 1967
and architect of the Likud political strategy, and, to the
shock of many Labourites, Moshe Dayan, who agreed to
become foreign minister. Begin also attracted the National
Religious Party to his coalition.

Menachem Begin

*(b. Aug. 16, 1913, Brest-Litovsk, Russia [now in Belarus]—d. March 9,
1992, Tel Aviv–Yafo, Israel)*

Menachem Begin was a Zionist leader who was prime minister of
Israel from 1977 to 1983. Begin was the co-recipient, with Egyptian
Pres. Anwar el-Sādāt, of the 1978 Nobel Prize for Peace for their
achievement of a peace treaty between Israel and Egypt that was formally signed in 1979.

Begin received a law degree from the University of Warsaw in 1935.
Active in the Zionist movement throughout the 1930s, he became
(1938) the leader of the Polish branch of the Betar youth movement,
dedicated to the establishment of a Jewish state on both sides of the
Jordan River. When the Germans invaded Warsaw in 1939, he escaped
to Vilnius; his parents and a brother died in concentration camps. The
Soviet authorities deported Begin to Siberia in 1940, but in 1941 he
was released and joined the Polish army in exile, with which he went
to Palestine in 1942.

Begin joined the militant Irgun Zvai Leumi and was its commander from 1943 to 1948. After Israel's independence in 1948 the

Irgun formed the Ḥerut ("Freedom") Party with Begin as its head and leader of the opposition in the Knesset until 1967. Begin joined the National Unity government (1967–70) as a minister without portfolio and in 1970 became joint chairman of the Likud ("Unity") coalition.

On May 17, 1977, the Likud Party won a national electoral victory and on June 21 Begin formed a government. He was perhaps best known for his uncompromising stand on the question of retaining the West Bank and the Gaza Strip, which had been occupied by Israel during the 1967 war. Prodded by U.S. Pres. Jimmy Carter, however, Begin negotiated with Pres. Anwar el-Sādāt of Egypt for peace in the Middle East, and the agreements they reached, known as the Camp David Accords (Sept. 17, 1978), led directly to a peace treaty between Israel and Egypt that was signed on March 26, 1979. Under the terms of the treaty, Israel returned the Sinai Peninsula, which it had occupied since the 1967 war, to Egypt in exchange for full diplomatic recognition. Begin and Sādāt were jointly awarded the Nobel Prize for Peace in 1978.

Menachem Begin, when he was commander of the Irgun Zvai Leumi. AFP/ Getty Images

Begin formed another coalition government after the general election of 1981. In spite of his willingness to return the Sinai Peninsula to Egypt under the terms of the peace agreement, he remained resolutely opposed to the establishment of a Palestinian state in the West Bank and Gaza Strip. In June 1982 his government mounted an invasion of Lebanon in an effort to oust the PLO from its bases there. The PLO was driven from Lebanon, but the deaths of numerous Palestinian civilians there turned world opinion against Israel. Israel's continuing involvement in Lebanon, and the death of Begin's wife in November 1982, were probably among the factors that prompted him to resign from office in October 1983.

THE BEGINNING OF THE PEACE PROCESS

Begin strongly opposed any territorial compromise on the West Bank, which, like many Israelis, he felt to be an inalienable part of Israel—the historic Samaria and Judea. He also argued that Resolution 242 did not require withdrawal from this area. The new Israeli leader put off a crisis with Washington by discarding Rabin's notion of "coordination" and declared simply that Israel wanted to sit down with its neighbours to negotiate peace. Meanwhile, Begin inaugurated a policy to strengthen Israel's hold on the West Bank through an extensive settlement program overseen by Ariel Sharon, the minister of agriculture.

Carter spent the summer in futile efforts to convene an international conference, finally approving a Soviet-American communiqué in October 1977 that was intended to stimulate diplomacy; instead, it outraged both Israel and the U.S. Congress, many of whose members condemned Carter for concessions to Moscow. These mishaps convinced Sādāt that American tactics were giving his erstwhile Soviet and Syrian allies a veto over any diplomacy, which could lead to a new war in which Egypt would likely pay the highest price. Secret negotiations were held between Israeli Foreign Minister Moshe Dayan and Sādāt's personal representatives, after which the Egyptian president surprised the world by flying to a delighted Israel in November 1977, where he and Begin addressed the Israeli Knesset.

The two leaders could not agree, however, on the details of a comprehensive peace, and the negotiations were complicated by events in Lebanon. Following its eviction from Jordan in 1971, the PLO had established itself there, exacerbating the volatile political situation in that country and contributing to its collapse into civil war in 1975. Both Israel and the United States had reluctantly consented to Syria's military intervention in Lebanon that same year, but the result was a partitioned state with the PLO dominating the south of the country, which was now a launching point for terror attacks against Israelis living in the Upper Galilee. In March 1978, Israel invaded Lebanon to drive the PLO away from the border but succeeded only partially in this goal before withdrawing from that country, under international pressure, in June. This episode strengthened Israel's ties with a Lebanese Christian militia known as the Phalange, who benefited from Israeli weapons and training.

CAMP DAVID

The faltering Egyptian-Israeli negotiations were finally rescued when Carter convened a summit at the presidential retreat of Camp David, Md., in September 1978. In this secluded site—an "elegant jail," Begin called it—Carter shuttled between the two leaders over a 12-day period, and out of these negotiations emerged the Camp David Accords. The accords were a framework for a comprehensive peace between Israel and the Arab states based on Resolution 242 and called for all the parties to complete peace treaties under its principles. Rather than giving the Palestinians full independence, the accords offered them Begin's concept of autonomy, which provided for a transitional period of not more than five years, during which time Israel, Egypt, Jordan, and the Palestinians would negotiate a permanent peace treaty to settle on the final status of the territories.

The Camp David Accords earned Sādāt and Begin each a share of the 1978 Nobel Prize for Peace, but the subsequent peace process proved far more difficult than the parties expected. It took seven more months for Egypt and Israel to reach a final agreement, which was signed on March 26, 1979, and called for a three-year phased Israeli withdrawal from the Sinai, limited-force zones, a multinational observer force, full diplomatic relations between the two countries, and special provisions for Israeli access to the Sinai's oil fields. The United States also agreed to provide large amounts of financial aid to both Israel and Egypt, part of which paid for the relocation of Israeli military installations. Israel's settlements in the Sinai were also evacuated, in spite of public Israeli protests.

Syria, Iraq, and the PLO were outraged by Egypt's actions and joined diplomatic forces to suspend Cairo from the Arab League and prevent any other Arab state from supporting the accords. Nearly all the Arab states subsequently severed ties with Egypt. Jordan and the Palestinians refused to negotiate autonomy, and a three-year attempt by Israel, Egypt, and the United States to develop the plan on their own came to naught. Meanwhile, Begin refused to halt the building of new Jewish settlements in the West Bank and Gaza Strip.

A COLD PEACE

Thus, "seven lean years" after the Yom Kippur War and three decades after independence, Israel had reached peace with Egypt, the Soviets were sidelined, and the Jewish state's alliance with the United States was consolidated. However, trouble loomed, as a civil war in Lebanon allowed an increasingly well-armed PLO to raid Israel's northern border. Israel had also begun to fear a military buildup in Iraq, especially its potential for producing nuclear weapons. Nor was the cabinet happy. Both Weizman and Dayan resigned from it, charging that the prime minister did not want to settle the Palestinian issue. The Begin government had also been much less successful in its domestic policies, and the economy, after a brief recovery in 1978–79, entered another inflationary spiral.

Israel faced a complex agenda in dealing with the United States when Ronald Reagan replaced Jimmy Carter as president in 1981. Reagan and his first secretary of state, Alexander Haig, both strong supporters of Israel, promoted a strategic alliance with the Jewish state, but the effort was soon beset by quarrels over the U.S. sale of sophisticated air surveillance aircraft, known as AWACS, to Saudi Arabia. When Israel destroyed Iraq's French-built Osirak nuclear reactor in a daring raid in June, Washington reluctantly supported a UN condemnation of Israel's action.

Begin's policies aroused strong international opposition but aided his victory over Shimon Peres in the June 1981 elections. His new government contained more Likud appointees, including Yitzhak Shamir as foreign minister and Ariel Sharon as defense minister. Then, on Oct. 6, 1981, Sādāt was murdered by Muslim extremists. His successor, Hosnī Mubārak, reaffirmed the 1979 treaty but was prepared only for a "cold" peace with Israel, and few of the bright hopes for trade and tourism promised by the Camp David agreements materialized—even after Israel completed its withdrawal from the Sinai in April 1982.

WAR IN LEBANON

Begin again turned to Lebanon, where he was determined to defeat the PLO. In July 1981, fearing an Israeli-Syrian clash in Lebanon, the United States had brokered an ambiguous cease-fire, during which the PLO continued to amass heavy arms. Cautioned by Haig not to attack unless there was an "internationally recognized provocation," Begin ordered the bombing of PLO positions in June 1982 after members of a PLO splinter group attempted to assassinate Israel's ambassador to Britain. The PLO retaliated with a rocket barrage on Israel's northern border towns, whereupon Israel launched a new invasion of southern Lebanon. The Israeli cabinet authorized a limited operation, and Begin made it clear that IDF troops were not to advance farther than 25 miles (40 km) beyond the Lebanese border. But Sharon had more ambitious plans. Even as Reagan's special envoy, Philip Habib, attempted to prevent an Israeli-Syrian clash, Israeli jets destroyed Syrian antiaircraft missiles in Lebanon. This strategic surprise attack was followed by a short but violent series of ground skirmishes and two days of aerial combat that cost Syria some 100 aircraft.

Sharon sent the IDF toward Beirut and well beyond the mandated 25-mile limit. With the Syrians in retreat, Israeli troops besieged 'Arafāt and his remaining PLO units in the Lebanese capital. Israel's Maronite Christian allies, the Phalange Party, contrary to Sharon's expectations, did not act to secure the city as they had been expected to do, and a dangerous stalemate ensued. The pro-Israel Haig was forced from office, as a bewildered and angry Reagan, reinforced by U.S. Secretary of Defense Caspar Weinberger, sought an Israeli withdrawal. Habib, working under the direction of Haig's successor, George

Shultz, managed to insert a multinational peacekeeping force in Lebanon that allowed 'Arafāt and a portion of his force to evacuate Beirut in August, following a final Israeli bombardment.

The Lebanese Christians, however, were not to benefit from the Israeli actions. Phalange leader Bashir Gemayel, the new president-elect, was assassinated by Syrian agents in September, and in the ensuing disorders, Israeli forces allowed the Phalangist militia into two Palestinian refugee camps, Sabra and Shatila, where they massacred hundreds (estimates vary between 700 and 3,000) of men, women, and children. The multinational force, withdrawn quickly after 'Arafāt's departure, was reinserted.

Shortly before the massacres, President Reagan had announced a plan for Arab-Israeli peace that pointedly applied the Resolution 242 formula to the Palestinian issue. The plan was designed, in part, to appease Arab anger and to revive the Jordanian option, but it was rejected by an Arab summit and hotly opposed by an alarmed Begin. However, the embattled prime minister did not have much time left. An official Israeli inquiry condemned Sharon for negligence in the camp massacres, forcing him to resign. Grieving over Israeli losses and the operation's tragic outcome, Israelis mounted massive street demonstrations against the Begin government.

Under U.S. mediation, Israel and Lebanon reached a nonbelligerence agreement in May 1983, and Israeli troops withdrew from the Beirut area. An ailing Begin, devastated by his wife's death and the war's outcome, resigned in September and retreated into a reclusive retirement, dying in 1992. He was replaced by Yitzhak Shamir. On Oct. 23, 1983, a suicide bomber from the radical Shī'ite Muslim organization Hezbollah blew up the U.S. Marine headquarters at the Beirut airport, which was part of the international peacekeeping force, killing 241. Within a few weeks, Reagan began withdrawing American forces, and after they had left, the Syrians and their local allies forced Lebanon to renounce the agreement with Israel.

THE NATIONAL UNITY GOVERNMENT

Labour outpolled the Likud in the 1984 election, but not by a margin sufficient to form a government. To rescue the economy and extricate Israel from its military entanglement in Lebanon, Labour and Likud formed a national unity government in September, giving the premiership to Peres for 25 months, at the end of which the premiership would go to Shamir, with the understanding that the other would take the position of deputy prime minister of foreign affairs. Notably, Rabin was to be defense minister for both men.

Under Peres, the Israelis began a phased withdrawal from Lebanon in June 1985, except for a security zone where an Israeli-sponsored Lebanese force waged intermittent warfare against the Hezbollah, who enjoyed Iranian and Syrian patronage. An economic recovery plan also was put into place, assisted by the United States. For the first time, Israel began to reform its economic structures, which until then had been controlled by the state and the labour federation, Histadrut.

As stipulated by the rotation agreement, Shamir became prime minister in October 1986, with Peres as foreign minister. Determined to regain the top spot through a diplomatic breakthrough, Peres met secretly with Jordan's King Hussein. The two reached an understanding known as the London Agreement in April 1987, but the agreement's vague formulations did not command a majority of votes in the unity cabinet, and Shamir retained control.

Shamir continued the Begin policy of settling Jews throughout the West Bank, hoping to isolate the Arab towns and villages that might form the basis for a Palestinian state. Few Israelis responded to this initiative until Sharon, who returned to Shamir's cabinet as housing minister, began subsidizing residential communities that were within easy commuting distance of Jerusalem and Tel Aviv, where housing was scarce and expensive. By 1992 the Jewish population in the occupied territories was approaching 100,000.

THE *INTIFĀḌAH*

The Begin and Shamir governments had gradually abandoned Moshe Dayan's old policy of leaving the Palestinians alone. By late 1987 the combined effects of settlement expansion, bureaucratic encroachment, land seizures,

Palestinian youths throw stones at Israeli soldiers during the first intifāḍah, *which began in the late 1980s.* AFP/Getty Images

several years of economic stagnation, and the diplomatic stalemate had set the stage for an Arab rebellion in the West Bank and Gaza that quickly became known as the *intifāḍah* (Arabic: "shaking off"). This uprising was distinguished by widespread street violence in which children and teenagers battled Israeli troops with rocks and stones.

The Israeli military was caught by surprise and proved ill-equipped to deal with the revolt. A grinding contest of wills ensued that soon claimed many civilian casualties and altered the political landscape. In February 1988 Shamir invited Secretary of State Shultz to intervene, but he tried in vain to revive the diplomatic process. Meanwhile, King Ḥussein had finally abandoned his formal ambition to represent the Palestinians. Israel's international image was suffering as the media recorded scenes of Israeli soldiers beating young Palestinians in the street. Frequent closures of the areas also severely disrupted the Palestinian economy, and Israel began to replace Arab day labour with immigrant workers from outside the region.

The Israeli election in November 1988 gave Likud a slight majority. Shamir was still forming a government when in December 'Arafāt, speaking at a special UN meeting in Geneva, reiterated a declaration that he had made the previous month that he was ready to recognize Israel and suspend terrorism provided the Palestinians obtained a state. The United States promptly recognized the PLO and opened a dialogue with it.

THE QUESTION OF PALESTINIAN AUTONOMY

This stunning event led Shamir to form another national unity government, with Rabin again as defense minister and Peres as finance minister. Rabin was convinced that Israel needed a political initiative to end the *intifāḍah* and deflect the PLO. He persuaded Shamir to revive the Camp

David-era autonomy plan, but this time it was stripped of its Jordanian component and aimed specifically at the Palestinians. Israel was also facing a new U.S. administration, led by Pres. George Bush, that was determined to restrict Israeli settlement expansion. Efforts by the United States to create an Israeli-Palestinian negotiation on autonomy, however, were rejected by Shamir, who insisted that the Palestinian negotiating team be drawn exclusively from residents of Gaza and the West Bank and not from Jerusalem or the PLO. Peres thereupon resigned from the unity government, only to be outmaneuvered by Shamir, who formed a Likud-dominated coalition that excluded Labour.

The prime minister decided to ride out the *intifāḍah* while concentrating on a sudden breakthrough with the Soviet Union. As part of Soviet leader Mikhail Gorbachev's reforms, a massive number of Soviet Jews were allowed to emigrate to Israel, the exodus continuing after the Russian Federation was created in the early 1990s. Included among the hundreds of thousands of new arrivals were many highly trained doctors, engineers, and scientists.

THE GULF WAR AND THE MADRID CONFERENCE

The stalemated Arab-Israeli conflict was soon overshadowed by a crisis in the Persian Gulf, when the army of Iraqi leader Ṣaddām Ḥussein invaded Kuwait in August 1990. As the United States dispatched troops to Saudi Arabia and organized an international coalition against the Iraqi invasion, Ṣaddām attempted to stir up Arab antagonism against Israel. He found ready support among the Palestinians in Jordan and elsewhere, including an endorsement by PLO head ʿArafāt.

The United States greatly feared that its focus on Iraqi aggression would be diverted by Arab grievances against

Israel, and when the American-led coalition's attack was launched, Washington urged Israel not to respond to Iraqi provocations, even after Iraqi forces began missile attacks on Israeli cities. Accepting U.S. air-defense missiles, Israel held its fire while the coalition devastated the Jewish state's most dangerous Arab opponent. Meanwhile, the Persian Gulf states cut off their previously substantial financial support for the PLO.

Iraq's defeat and the rapid decline of the Soviet Union in 1991 suddenly opened the way for fresh diplomatic initiatives. U.S. Secretary of State James Baker succeeded in convening an Arab-Israeli peace conference in Madrid in October 1991, the first direct official talks between Israel and its neighbours since the Camp David era. Three "tracks" were created under U.S. auspices: achievement of peace treaties between Israel and Jordan, Lebanon, and Syria; the creation of an interim Palestinian self-government for Gaza and the West Bank (the Palestinian team this time met the Israeli specifications); and gaining European, Japanese, and Arab support for regional economic cooperation and arms control.

The talks, conducted in various locations, stalled after a promising start. The Palestinians demanded statehood rather than autonomy, and Shamir was not interested in reaching quick agreements. The Israeli leader remained faithful to his strategy of outlasting the other side while continuing to construct Israeli settlements in the West Bank and Gaza. However, Shamir's policy was hotly contested by the United States, and Bush refused Shamir's request for housing-loan guarantees to accommodate Russian immigrants unless Israel stopped expanding the settlements.

The Labour opposition, sensing an opportunity, put up Rabin as their candidate for prime minister in the elections of June 1992. He promised security but also flexibility, insisting that he would produce progress in the negotiations. He also proposed that less be spent on settlements and more on help for Russian immigrants. In a hard-fought election, the Labour Party won a narrow advantage.

THE RABIN GOVERNMENT

Rabin established greater control in this premiership than in his earlier one by keeping the defense portfolio to himself and appointing a negotiating team that reported to him rather than to Peres, his foreign minister. His coalition was delicately balanced between left and right and relied on a Sephardic religious party, Shas, to offset the strongly antireligious Meretz Party.

Rabin criticized the comprehensive approach implicit in the Madrid talks, concluding that the Palestinian-Israeli track held more promise for progress because both Israelis and Palestinians wanted to move beyond the status quo of the *intifādah*. To stimulate diplomacy and to patch up relations with the United States, he ordered a freeze on the construction of Israeli settlements in the occupied territories, which allowed the Bush administration to approve housing guarantees for Russian immigrants. (In fact, some previously planned construction continued in the territories, and the settler population grew from 100,000 to 135,000 during Rabin's term.)

Unexpectedly, the negotiations with Syria came to life first, but after an encouraging start they had deadlocked by the summer of 1993. Syria refused to specify what it meant by "full peace," a key Israeli requirement; and Israel refused to withdraw to the armistice lines as they were prior to the 1967 war, which would have effectively placed the border with Syria on Lake Tiberias, Israel's largest source of fresh water.

Shas

Shas (Hebrew, in full: Sephardim Shomrei Torah; English: Sephardi Torah Guardians) is an ultra-Orthodox religious political party in Israel.

Shas was founded in 1984 by dissident members of the Ashkenazi-dominated Agudat Israel, another ultrareligious party, to represent the interests of religiously observant Sephardic Jews. The Sephardim, including many who were not religiously observant, were attracted to the party, particularly in the 1990s, because they saw it as a way to voice their grievances concerning discrimination in education, employment, and housing. In 1984 Shas won four seats in the Knesset, and it marginally increased its representation in 1988 to six seats, a success attributed largely to its participation in a unity government until 1987. While in government it was given control of the Interior Ministry, which allowed it to funnel money to services for religious Sephardic Jews. Broadening its appeal to secular Sephardim, Shas won 10 seats in 1996, and by the late 1990s it was the third largest party in the Knesset, challenging the status of the Israel Labour Party and Likud, traditionally the country's two largest parties, and acting as a power broker in coalition negotiations. Although Shas's standing in the Knesset slipped to fifth with 11 seats after the 2009 election, in general the party won substantial and fairly consistent representation in the Knesset during the 2000s. It has entered coalition governments with both Labour and Likud.

Shas policy is determined by a council of sages. Seeking to expand the funding of religious institutions, Shas has focused much of its policy attention on social services and education. It also has opposed efforts to further secularize Israel, particularly proposals to introduce civil marriage. Shas has equivocated on the peace accords signed between Israel and the Palestinians in the 1990s; with the exception of East Jerusalem, Shas has steadfastly opposed the building of Israeli settlements in areas conquered by Israel in 1967, and, though it supports autonomy for the Palestinians, Shas has opposed the establishment of a Palestinian state.

THE OSLO ACCORDS

Meanwhile, Peres had been nurturing a secret negotiating track with the Palestinians through Norwegian diplomacy. The PLO officials conducting the so-called unofficial discussions in Oslo were far more flexible than the official non-PLO Palestinian delegation in Washington, and Rabin decided to gamble that 'Arafāt was the only Palestinian leader who could conceivably deliver peace. 'Arafāt also gambled. He was short of money after alienating his main financial backers during the Gulf War and faced challenges to his leadership from Islamic groups, whose influence had grown significantly in the occupied territories during the *intifāḍah*. He accepted the idea of Palestinian autonomy in order to at last obtain a foothold in Palestine.

THE DECLARATION OF PRINCIPLES AND CAIRO AGREEMENT

In September 1993, Israel and the PLO signed the Declaration of Principles on Palestinian Self-Rule, the first agreement between the two sides and the initial document in what became generally known as the Oslo Accords. While the United States had not been aware of the seriousness of the discussions in Oslo, both Rabin and 'Arafāt were happy to embrace U.S. Pres. Bill Clinton on the White House lawn in September 1993, in support of their deal. A visibly reluctant Rabin consented to shake 'Arafāt's hand.

The Oslo Accords, in fact, comprised a series of agreements, the second of which, the Cairo Agreement on the Gaza Strip and Jericho, was signed in May 1994. This pact enacted the provisions set forth in the original declaration, which had endorsed a five-year interim self-rule for a Palestinian authority to be executed in two stages: first in Gaza and the city of Jericho and then, after an election, throughout the remaining areas under Israeli military rule. Talks on final status were to begin after three years, with a two-year deadline for an agreement to be reached. Issues such as borders, the return of refugees, the status of Jerusalem, and Jewish settlements in the occupied territories were reserved for final status talks. The PLO recognized Israel's right to exist, renounced terrorism, and agreed to change the portions of its charter that called for Israel's destruction. Israel recognized the PLO as the sole representative of the Palestinian people.

The accords embodied two basic sets of exchanges. First, Israel would shed responsibility for the Palestinian population while retaining strategic control of the territory. The Palestinians would be rid of Israeli military rule and gain self-government, potentially leading to statehood. Second, 'Arafāt's disavowal of violence and his pledge to fight terrorism—through the use of a domestic Palestinian police force—would improve Israel's security. The Palestinians would benefit from the large amount of foreign aid it would receive from the United States and other countries and from economic agreements made with Israel that were designed to foster employment and trade.

CHALLENGES TO PEACE

Rabin's decision aroused enormous opposition from the Likud and most settlers, although the majority of Israelis at first strongly supported him, especially since the agreement enabled Israel to rid itself of the tumultuous Gaza Strip. In October 1994, Jordan also signed a comprehensive peace treaty with Israel, and many other Arab states, including the smaller Persian Gulf emirates, began to discard the old taboos about contact with the Jewish state.

Not all Palestinians, however, favoured 'Arafāt's course. Ḥamās, which was especially strong in Gaza,

violently opposed the Oslo Accords and launched a series
of terror attacks on Israeli civilians, killing scores between
1993 and 1997. Rabin retaliated with border closures that
prevented tens of thousands of Palestinian workers living in the occupied territories from commuting to jobs in
Israel. Some Israelis sought revenge, such as the murder
in February 1994 of some three dozen Arabs at prayer in
Hebron's Tomb of the Patriarchs by an Israeli settler. In
spite of Israeli protests, 'Arafāt sought to co-opt rather
than repress Ḥamās. Israel therefore continued its own
antiterrorism war, and two Ḥamās leaders were assassinated in 1994–95, one in Gaza itself.

Economic Boom

Peace diplomacy bolstered what had already been a period
of strong economic expansion in Israel. Austerity during
the 1980s had wrung out bad debt and inefficiency at considerable cost. Many kibbutzim, deprived of cheap credit
and a subsidized water supply, had either failed or shifted
from agriculture to light industry. Koor Industries Ltd.,
Histadrut's industrial holding company, had itself fallen
on hard times and defaulted on a number of loans before it
was restructured. The Israeli government still controlled
half the economy, but the earlier socialist ideology, once
the mainstay of Israeli politics, was clearly on the wane.

In the late 1980s the Israeli economy was buoyed by the
influx of highly skilled Russian immigrants, a competitive
high-technology sector, and the country's proximity to the
European market. In the period 1990–95, Israel's rate of
economic growth exceeded 5 percent annually, unemployment was cut nearly in half, and the annual inflation rate
dropped from double to single digits. Foreign investment
turned from a trickle into a flood, as Israeli exports to Asia
also registered large increases and the Arab boycott eased.

By 1996 Israel's GNP was greater than that of Jordan, Syria, and Lebanon combined, and its per capita income was approaching European standards. All this made Israel an economic powerhouse in the region and allowed its leaders to look at a future of decreasing dependence on economic aid from the United States.

OSLO II AND RABIN'S ASSASSINATION

In September 1995, Rabin, 'Arafāt, and Peres, all newly named winners of the Nobel Prize for Peace, assembled again on the White House lawn to sign the Interim Agreement on the West Bank and Gaza Strip (often called Oslo II). This detailed and long-delayed agreement established a schedule for Israeli withdrawals from the Palestinian population centres (to be implemented in several stages) and created a complex system of zones that were divided between areas fully controlled by the Palestinians, those under Palestinian civil authority but Israeli military control, and those exclusively under Israeli control. It also set elections for a president and council of the PA, which would govern the Palestinian population in the occupied territories.

Although Oslo I had received strong parliamentary support, Oslo II was ratified by only one vote in the Knesset, signaling a significant loss of support for Rabin. Many Israelis were angry over 'Arafāt's erratic cooperation on security, and others, especially the Likud—now led by Israel's former ambassador to the UN, Benjamin Netanyahu—hotly opposed withdrawals or further dealings with 'Arafāt. Meanwhile, the Sephardic Shas Party had left the coalition in protest over the indictment of its parliamentary leader for fraud. Bereft of his coalition's balance, Rabin had to depend on the vote of the Israeli Arab members of the Knesset for his majority. He was also battered by demands from the Meretz Party and from Conservative and Reform Jews in the United States to loosen the Orthodox religious monopoly established in the early years of the state.

Shortly after Oslo II was passed in the Knesset, Rabin decided on a public campaign to rally his supporters, and it was following the first such rally in Tel Aviv in November 1995 that he was assassinated by a Jewish religious fanatic. Israelis were horrified. After a funeral attended by many international leaders, including Arabs, a round of soul-searching and recriminations began. Popular Israeli support for the peace process surged, and with the Likud on the defensive, Shimon Peres, Rabin's successor as prime minister, proceeded with Oslo II.

By early 1996 nearly all the Palestinians were under self-rule. Israeli forces, though withdrawn from the major towns except Hebron, still controlled most of the

Israeli Prime Minister Yitzhak Rabin (right) *voices his support for Oslo II, while Shimon Peres listens in. A month after it was passed in the Knesset, Rabin was assassinated.* Sven Nackstrand/AFP/Getty Images

occupied territories. In January, 'Arafāt easily won election as president of the PA. The voters also selected a Palestinian Council, although its powers were ill-defined. Peres also sought to accelerate an Israeli-Syrian deal but soon concluded that such an agreement could not be reached quickly, if at all.

A NEW POLITICAL LANDSCAPE

Peres had hoped to capitalize on sympathy for Rabin and chose to hold early elections in 1996. His campaign was quickly upset by a series of Ḥamās suicide attacks against civilians that shocked and angered Israelis. The United States convened an international antiterrorism conference in March to support Peres, but the prime minister lacked Rabin's security credentials and had been an outspoken advocate of partnership with 'Arafāt. Peres reacted to Hezbollah attacks along the Lebanese border by ordering a massive artillery bombardment of southern Lebanon that mistakenly hit a UN outpost sheltering hundreds of civilians, which damaged his standing among Israeli Arabs. In addition, Labour had lost popularity among religious voters because of its alliance with Meretz.

THE NETANYAHU PREMIERSHIP

The May elections were the first held under a new law that allowed separate ballots for prime minister and the Knesset, which was designed to reduce the ability of smaller parties to exact concessions when governments were formed. However, this law had the opposite result: it created a quasi-presidential regime that still depended on an increasingly fractured parliament. Peres narrowly lost to Netanyahu, who promised that he would be tougher on 'Arafāt than Peres had been. In the Knesset, however, both Labour and Likud unexpectedly lost ground, while the smaller parties, especially the religious bloc, gained large numbers of seats. An ethnic Russian party, Yisrael B'Aliyah, led by the celebrated Soviet-era dissident Anatoly (Natan) Sharansky, also won seats. The growth of the Shas Party and the emergence of a Russian ethnic bloc offered compelling evidence not only of their grievances against previous governments but of the failure of the major political parties to integrate these constituencies.

Netanyahu, age 46, the first Israeli prime minister born after the founding of the state, promised to accelerate economic reforms, especially the sale of state-owned businesses, but he was quickly confronted by labour union opposition, a slowing economy, and a large budget deficit. He had been a severe critic of the Oslo Accords but, after Rabin's murder, had promised to fix the agreements by insisting on Palestinian "reciprocity" (i.e., strict adherence to the terms). Nonetheless, Netanyahu could not bring himself to meet 'Arafāt until September 1996 and raised doubts over his willingness to proceed with the promised Israeli withdrawal from Hebron and other unfinished aspects of Oslo II.

CRISIS IN THE PEACE PROCESS

'Arafāt had finally acted against Ḥamās in the spring and summer of 1996, but Israel's surprise opening of an archaeological tunnel exit at the north end of the Western Wall in Jerusalem in September 1996 allowed 'Arafāt to play on Palestinian fears that the tunnel was a threat to Al-Aqṣā Mosque. Another violent round of protests ensued, in which Palestinian police fired on Israeli soldiers, killing more than a dozen, while some 60 Arabs died. Clinton, fearing the end of the peace process, called an emergency summit in the White House, after which the Israeli prime minister warmly shook 'Arafāt's hand for the cameras. Netanyahu refused to close the tunnel, but he pledged an accelerated effort to negotiate an agreement on the West Bank city of Hebron, which was reached in January 1997.

Netanyahu's cabinet narrowly approved the Hebron Agreement. Part of the price for this action became clear when Israel began constructing a long-planned but often delayed Jewish neighbourhood on the outskirts of Jerusalem, which would effectively cut off the Arab villages on the eastern side of the city from the rest of the West Bank. 'Arafāt held his protest of this project until the cabinet's decision on the first of three projected Israeli withdrawals in March. When these withdrawals turned out to be far less significant than 'Arafāt had anticipated, the stage was set for another round of protests that quickly escalated into violence. Meanwhile, 'Arafāt released Ḥamās activists from Palestinian jails and suspended security cooperation with Israel. Netanyahu, fearing that his cabinet would not approve any more interim steps, argued that Israel and the Palestinians should begin intensive negotiations to determine the final status of the territories. This proposal was quickly rejected by both 'Arafāt and the United States.

THE WYE RIVER MEMORANDUM

The breakdown of direct Israeli-Palestinian negotiation at high levels led the United States to intervene again in early 1998 to end the stalemate. Both sides met in rural Maryland in October, and after intensive negotiations that included President Clinton's active participation produced the Wye River Memorandum. The new agreement restored old Israeli promises (such as the opening of a Palestinian airport and a safe passage route between Gaza and the West Bank) for old Palestinian promises (such as publicly renouncing the PLO Charter's anti-Israel provisions, collecting unauthorized arms, and implementing antiterrorism actions), but its novelty consisted of linking phased Israeli withdrawals to Palestinian actions and greatly enlarging the role of the United States as an active participant in both monitoring and judging the performance of the parties. Wye promised to put two-fifths of the West Bank under partial or total Palestinian control.

Netanyahu returned from Wye to face growing political trouble. The Bank of Israel had been using high interest rates in a dramatic effort to reduce Israeli inflation. While the policy succeeded overall (the inflation rate was cut by two-thirds) it also precipitated a recession and rising unemployment, which hit hardest in the poorer sectors of society—notably the largely Sephardic residents of the development towns in the south. Concurrently, the government's budget had been reduced, which hampered the prime minister's ability to satisfy the demands of the various coalition members. In early 1999, after a legislative defeat on the budget, Netanyahu called for early elections and soon suspended the Wye agreement.

THE BARAK GAMBLE

The May 1999 Israeli election produced an even more fractured Knesset than the one three years earlier. Whereas in 1992, under the old, purely parliamentary system, the two largest parties had between them won 76 of the 120 seats, by 1999 they could command only 45. Labour, renamed One Israel in coalition with two small parties, had the most seats in the Knesset, while Likud, beset by infighting and a stalled economy, was second. The real surprise of the election was the sudden growth of Shas, which now commanded the third-largest number of seats.

Labour's candidate for prime minister was a retired general, Ehud Barak, who triumphed over Netanyahu by a decisive margin. Barak, the most decorated soldier in Israeli history, had promised a renewed drive for peace, economic growth, and resistance to religious demands. He assembled a broad coalition in the Knesset and set about reviving the peace process with both the Palestinians and Syrians with a certain sense of urgency—'Arafāt had already threatened to declare a Palestinian state unilaterally at the time of the Wye summit, Syrian Pres. Ḥāfiẓ al-Assad was seriously ill (he died in June 2000), and President Clinton wished to achieve a peace agreement before the end of his term in office.

In Barak's view, new elements existed that made rapid progress toward peace possible on both the Syrian and Palestinian fronts. Like his predecessor, he wanted definitive talks with 'Arafāt about the final status of the territories before vacating much more land, but he encountered heavy resistance to his plans from both foreign and domestic sources. The Palestinians would not agree to abandon the third and final troop withdrawal promised under Oslo II. 'Arafāt put off the declaration of a Palestinian state but insisted on maximum American intervention and sought the most territory he could recover before the final negotiations. However, he did agree to Barak's deadline of Feb. 15, 2000, to reach a framework agreement, which was to be preceded by another withdrawal. These new arrangements were incorporated in the so-called Wye II agreement, reached in September 1999. None of the deadlines was met.

As the prime minister expected and 'Arafāt feared, the Syrians suddenly signaled their desire to negotiate in early December. Barak himself traveled to the United States to negotiate with Syrian Foreign Minister Fārūq al-Sharʿ, under Clinton's patronage. A second session in early January 2000, however, ended when Syrian President Assad broke off the talks, raising the old demand that Israel agree to a return to the borders that existed between the two countries before the Six-Day War as a precondition to further negotiations.

By early March, however, progress again seemed possible on the Syrian front. Assad agreed to a summit with

President Clinton at Geneva, but to U.S. and Israeli surprise he yet again insisted on Syria's right to its pre-1967 positions on Lake Tiberias. Neither Barak nor a majority of Israelis would agree to this demand. Barak then carried out his campaign promise to withdraw Israeli troops from Lebanon, even without an agreement with Syria, to a border demarcated by the UN.

Barak's willingness to concede to Arab demands and his mishandling of his coalition destroyed his Knesset majority in June. Nonetheless, he decided to attend Clinton's hastily arranged summit at Camp David in July. This last-ditch effort to reach an agreement between 'Arafāt and Barak had been resisted by the Palestinian leader, who stated ahead of time that he could not concede Palestinian rights. This proved to be the case. Barak's unexpected willingness to share Jerusalem with the Palestinians was not reciprocated by 'Arafāt, who on this—as on the issue of the return of refugees—refused to compromise, demanding nothing less than full Palestinian sovereignty in East Jerusalem.

THE SECOND *INTIFĀDAH*

'Arafāt returned home from the summit to Palestinian and popular Arab acclaim. He had said "no" to both Israel and the United States. In contrast, Barak's political support evaporated. As he struggled to survive, a new blow fell when the Palestinians erupted in violence following a visit by Likud leader Sharon to the Temple Mount in September to promote Israeli sovereignty over the site. Rioting by Israeli Arabs further disturbed the situation. As international efforts to restore peace failed, cameras recorded the death of a 12-year-old Arab boy by gunfire in Gaza, and not long thereafter two Israeli soldiers were lynched in the West Bank. By spring 2001, hundreds had been killed, most of them Palestinians. President Clinton made one last attempt to bridge the gap, but neither side accepted his "parameters."

The failure of the Camp David summit and the outbreak of what came to be known as the Aqṣā *intifāḍah* convinced a majority of Israelis that they lacked a partner in 'Arafāt to end the conflict. Barak paid the political price, losing the premiership to Sharon by nearly 25 percent of the vote in elections held in February 2001. Sharon formed a broadly based coalition government.

The violence continued and escalated, even though Sharon in late 2003 announced a "disengagement plan" that called for Israel to withdraw its soldiers and remove Israeli settlers from the Gaza Strip and parts of the West Bank. The death of 'Arafāt in late 2004 paved the way for Israel and a more moderate Palestinian leadership to resume negotiations, and a cease-fire was agreed to in early 2005 that reduced significantly the level of violence. In spite of considerable opposition to Sharon's disengagement plan within Likud, Israel completed its pullout in September 2005. Sharon by then was weary of party infighting and, with other Likud moderates, formed the centrist Kadima ("Forward") Party in November. He fell victim to a debilitating stroke in early 2006, just before parliamentary elections, and Ehud Olmert became acting prime minister.

Kadima

Kadima (English: Forward) is a centrist Israeli political party formed in November 2005 by Israeli prime minister Ariel Sharon following his split from the Likud Party. When his policy of unilateral disengagement from the Gaza Strip and certain West Bank settlements encountered opposition from within Likud, Sharon decided to form a centre-oriented alternative to both the right-wing Likud and the social-democratic Israel Labour Party. A number of prominent members of

Likud (e.g., Ehud Olmert, a former mayor of Jerusalem, and Tzipi Livni, Israel's minister of justice) and a smaller number from Labour (e.g., former prime minister Shimon Peres) left their parties to join Kadima.

After Sharon suffered a debilitating stroke in January 2006, Olmert became acting prime minister and assumed leadership of the party. In the March 2006 general election, the first in which Kadima participated, the party secured 29 Knesset seats. After forming a coalition that included Labour-Meimad (a partnership between Labour and Meimad, a moderate religious group; 19 seats), Pensioners' Party (7 seats), and Shas (12 seats), Olmert was confirmed as prime minister in May. He promised to continue Sharon's policies of disengagement from Israeli-occupied areas and of setting permanent borders between Israel and the Palestinians by 2010.

As time passed, Olmert faced multiple allegations of corruption, and calls for his resignation mounted. In July 2008 he announced that he would step down following party elections scheduled for later that year. In September 2008 Livni (since March 2006, Israel's minister of foreign affairs) was elected to lead Kadima, and Olmert formally resigned. Livni was unable to piece together a governing coalition, however, so Olmert remained acting prime minister, and general elections were called for February 2009. Although Kadima won 28 seats (one more than Likud), because of the close and inconclusive nature of the results, it was not immediately clear whether Livni or Benjamin Netanyahu—the head of Likud since Sharon's departure from that party in 2005—would be invited to form a coalition government. Through the course of coalition discussions in the days that followed, Netanyahu gathered the support of Yisrael Beiteinu (15 seats), Shas (11 seats), and a number of smaller parties, and he was asked by Israel's president to form the government.

Kadima was founded on the basis of a centrist ideology. It supports dialogue with the Palestinians, a two-state solution, and a policy of territorial concession to retain a Jewish majority in Israel.

Kadima under Olmert won the largest share of Knesset seats. His stated goals were to withdraw more Israeli troops and settlers from the West Bank and finalize Israel's borders by 2010. However, the unexpected victory by Ḥamās in Palestinian elections earlier in 2006 brought a new uncertainty to Israeli-Palestinian relations, as did the Ḥamās takeover of the Gaza Strip in 2007. Israel recognized the West Bank administration, led by the more moderate Palestinian organization Fatah, as the legitimate Palestinian government and later declared the Gaza Strip under Ḥamās a hostile entity and implemented a series of sanctions. Ḥamās attacks on Israel continued, as did Israeli retaliatory strikes and attacks aimed at Ḥamās militants.

After months of negotiations, in June 2008 Israel and Ḥamās agreed to implement a truce scheduled to last six months. However, this was threatened shortly thereafter as each accused the other of violations, which escalated in the last months of the agreement. When the truce officially expired on December 19, Ḥamās announced that they did not intend to extend it. Broader hostilities erupted shortly thereafter as Israel, responding to sustained rocket fire, mounted a series of air strikes across the region—among the strongest in years—meant to target Ḥamās. After a week of air strikes, Israeli forces initiated a ground campaign into the Gaza Strip amid calls from the international community for a cease-fire. Following more than three weeks of hostilities—in which perhaps more than 1,000 were killed and tens of thousands left homeless—Israel and Ḥamās each declared a unilateral cease-fire.

Meanwhile, conflict with Hezbollah in neighbouring Lebanon was also an ongoing challenge. The abduction of two Israeli soldiers by Hezbollah in mid-2006 sparked a controversial 34-day war on Lebanese soil in which Israel failed to free its soldiers or eradicate Hezbollah, and the war, in which more than 1,000 Lebanese and more than 150 Israelis were killed, drew both domestic and international reproach. Although the final report, issued in January 2008 by the Winograd Commission (a body of inquiry convened to investigate the conduct of the July 2006 campaign), was highly critical of the upper echelons of Israeli political and military leadership, its appraisal of Olmert in particular was not as harsh as some had anticipated.

Olmert's public standing was further weakened, however, by allegations of corruption, the most high-profile of which alleged that he had accepted large sums of money from an American businessman before his tenure as prime minister. In the course of the subsequent inquiry, Olmert argued that the contributions were used to legally finance his election campaign, but he pledged to step down if charged. Calls for his resignation mounted as the inquiry progressed, and in July 2008 Olmert announced that he would step down after party elections scheduled for the fall of that year. In the September election, one of Olmert's rivals, Tzipi Livni, emerged as the leader of Kadima. As promised, Olmert formally resigned, although he remained leader of an interim government until a new prime minister could be selected. Livni was unable to form a coalition government, however, and elections were called for February 2009.

Although the election results indicated that Livni's Kadima had secured one Knesset seat more than Netanyahu's Likud, neither party had attained a majority, and the narrow margin of the results made it unclear which party leader would ultimately be invited to form a governing coalition. Through the course of coalition discussions in the days that followed, Netanyahu gathered the support of Yisrael Beiteinu (15 seats), Shas (11 seats), and a number of smaller parties, and he was asked by Israel's president to form the government.

A CHANGING SOCIETY

As the 21st century began, Israel was poised on the brink of significant change. At home the Israelis found themselves grappling with both perennial and new problems that included not only the old issue of religion and state and how these institutions relate to Jewish identity but also new pressures to reduce religious influence over personal matters such as marriage and divorce and to allow non-Orthodox rabbis to conduct these and other religious ceremonies—raising the very issue of who may legitimately be called a rabbi. Likewise, Israel faced the question of how to assimilate more than 250,000 non-Jews who had been part of the Russian emigration, raising the question of how one becomes a Jew. No less problematic was the issue of a large Arab minority that continued to assert its rights and demand equality in a Jewish state.

On the economic front, Israel had only partially completed its transformation from a socialist state into a more competitive market system by the end of the 20th century. Israel's military, long a unifying social institution, not only needed to counter new dangers from states such as Iraq and especially Iran—whose quest for nuclear capabilities was a particular concern in light of its anti-Israeli rhetoric—but also had to face the difficulties of changing to a more technical, less manpower-intensive force. Likewise, the political system badly needed reform following the failed experiment with direct elections for prime minister. Against this list of challenges, Israel could marshal its large and highly trained workforce, a dynamic technical sector, a large per capita gross national product, a record of absorbing large groups of immigrants, and a powerful army.

CONCLUSION

The region long revered as the Holy Land holds an especially esteemed position in each of the world's three major monotheistic religions. Numerous locales of historical, spiritual, and cultural significance are found there, and some deeply treasured sites are shared to varying extents by multiple religious communities. The region's significance is also bound up in the legacy of the Arab-Israeli conflict—easily among the most complex and most divisive territorial disputes in modern times, and a theme that has dominated the course of regional history for decades.

With the establishment of the state of Israel in 1948, a new political reality was crystallized within the region, and the statuses of Palestinian and Jewish communities there took on new meaning. In succeeding years, the Arab-Israeli conflict and its host of attendant issues—including the fate of Palestinian refugees, the status of the city of Jerusalem, terrorism, settlements, freedom of movement, naming and identity, and access to everything from basic resources to sacred sites—have exerted a polarizing effect between (and within) countries throughout the world. The conflict has attained such a broad reach that it now effects a defining influence on foreign policy and political decisionmaking in countries both inside and outside the region.

Within Israel and among Jewish communities abroad, opinions on the conflict and its many facets have been wide-ranging and frequently heated. Within the Palestinian community, ideological conflict between competing Fatah and Ḥamās leaderships has sent the West Bank and Gaza Strip ever further adrift from one another, casting the future of a unified Palestinian leadership into uncertainty. At the end of the first decade of the 21st century, meaningful steps toward Palestinian autonomy had been achieved, but there remained no sovereign Palestinian state. Thus, more than six decades after the establishment of the State of Israel, the ultimate status of the region and its inhabitants remains unclear.

GLOSSARY

assimilate To absorb into the culture or mores of a population or group.

autonomy The quality or state of being self-governing.

citadel A fortress that commands a city; a stronghold.

Diaspora The dispersion of Jews among outside Palestine after the Babylonian Exile; or the aggregate of Jews or Jewish communities scattered outside Palestine or present-day Israel.

emirate The state or jurisdiction of an emir, who is a ruler, chief, or commander in Islamic countries.

entente An international understanding providing for a common course of action.

Hellenistic Of or relating to Greek history, culture, or art after Alexander the Great.

ibex A sturdy species of wild goat found in the mountains of Europe, Asia, and northeastern Africa.

intifāḍah An uprising of Palestinians against Israeli occupation of the West Bank and Gaza Strip.

jihad Arabic term that has come to denote any conflict waged for principle or belief, although it also signifies any internal struggle related to the practice of Islam; often translated to mean "holy war."

kibbutz Israeli communal settlement in which all wealth is held in common and profits are reinvested in the settlement.

Knesset The parliament of Israel and supreme authority of that state.

legion A military organization, originally the largest permanent organization in the armies of ancient Rome.

maquis Scrubland vegetation of the Mediterranean region, composed primarily of leathery, broad-leaved evergreen shrubs or small trees.

nomad A person who has no permanent home and
instead moves about from place to place.

ombudsman A government official who investigates
other government officials when citizens complain of
bureaucratic abuse.

Semitic Of, relating to, or constituting a subgroup of
Afro-Asiatic cultures whose language group includes
Arabic, Hebrew, Amharic, and Aramaic.

sheruts Privately owned and operated shuttles that transport people in Israel.

unicameral Having or consisting of a single legislative
chamber; Israel's Knesset is a unicameral legislature.

Zionism A Jewish nationalism movement with the goal
of establishing a Jewish state in Palestine.

BIBLIOGRAPHY

Physical and human geography of Palestine is discussed in Ewan W. Anderson, *The Middle East: Geography and Geopolitics* (2000). Also of interest is *An Atlas on Palestine: The West Bank and Gaza* (2000).

The multivolume *Cambridge Ancient History* provides an authoritative survey of Palestine in all periods of antiquity. Prehistory and early history are examined by William Foxwell Albright, *The Archaeology of Palestine*, rev. ed. (1954, reprinted 1971); Archaeological Institute of America, *Archaeological Discoveries in the Holy Land* (1967); A.T. Olmstead, *History of Palestine and Syria to the Macedonian Conquest* (1931, reissued 1972); Michael Grant, *The History of Ancient Israel* (1984, reissued 1997); John Bright, *A History of Israel*, 4th ed. (2000); Kathleen M. Kenyon, *Archaeology in the Holy Land*, 4th ed. (1979, reprinted 1985); and F.E. Peters, *Jerusalem: The Holy City in the Eyes of Chroniclers, Visitors, Pilgrims, and Prophets from the Days of Abraham to the Beginnings of Modern Times* (1985, reissued 1995).

Hellenistic and Roman Palestine are the subject of Victor Tcherikover, *Hellenistic Civilization and the Jews*, trans. from Hebrew (1959, reprinted 1999); M. Rostovtzeff, *The Social & Economic History of the Hellenistic World*, 3 vol. (1941, reprinted 1986); and A.H.M. Jones, *The Herods of Judaea* (1938, reissued 1967). The most valuable multivolume general modern work is Emil Schürer, *The History of the Jewish People in the Age of Jesus Christ (175 B.C.–A.D. 135)*, rev. and ed. by Geza Vermes and Fergus Millar, trans. by T.A. Burkill et al. from German (1973–). Other useful works are E. Mary Smallwood, *The Jews Under Roman Rule: From Pompey to Diocletian* (1976, reprinted 1981); and Michael Avi-Yonah, *The Jews of Palestine: A Political History from the Bar Kokhba War to the Arab Conquest*, trans. from

Hebrew (1976; reprinted as *The Jews Under Roman and Byzantine Rule*, 1984).

Studies of the periods of Muslim rule in Palestine before 1516 include Guy Le Strange (trans.), *Palestine Under the Moslems: A Description of Syria and the Holy Land from A.D. 650 to 1500* (1890, reprinted 1975), a collection of medieval Arabic sources; K.J. Asali (ed.), *Jerusalem in History* (1989, reprinted 2000); and Amnon Cohen and Gabriel Baer (eds.), *Egypt and Palestine: A Millennium of Association (868–1948)* (1984).

Among many works on Ottoman Palestine, the following are among the broadest and most valuable: Beshara Doumani, *Rediscovering Palestine: Merchants and Peasants in Jabal Nablus, 1700–1900*, (1995); Alexander Schölch, *Palestine in Transformation, 1856–1882* (1993; originally published in German, 1986); Moshe Ma'oz (ed.), *Studies on Palestine During the Ottoman Period* (1975); Amnon Cohen, *Palestine in the 18th Century: Patterns of Government and Administration* (1973); David Kushner (ed.), *Palestine in the Late Ottoman Period: Political, Social, and Economic Transformation* (1986); Gershon Shafir, *Land, Labor and the Origins of the Israeli-Palestinian Conflict, 1882–1914*, updated ed. (1996); and Neville J. Mandel, *The Arabs and Zionism Before World War I* (1976, reissued 1980).

Some useful general studies that cover Palestine in the 20th century are Edward W. Said, *The Question of Palestine* (1979, reissued 1992); Samih K. Farsoun and Christina E. Zacharia, *Palestine and the Palestinians* (1997); Baruch Kimmerling and Joel S. Migdal, *Palestinians: The Making of a People* (1993); Fred J. Khouri, *The Arab-Israeli Dilemma*, 3rd ed. (1985); Howard M. Sachar, *A History of Israel*, 2 vol. (1976–87); Rosemary Sayigh, *Palestinians: From Peasants to Revolutionaries* (1979), a collection of interviews with camp Palestinians in Lebanon; Bruce R. Kuniholm and Michael Rubner, *The Palestinian Problem and United States Policy: A*

Guide to Issues and References (1986), with an extensive bibliography; Michael W. Suleiman (ed.), *U.S. Policy on Palestine: From Wilson to Clinton* (1995); Muhammad Y. Muslih, *The Origins of Palestinian Nationalism* (1988); Pamela Ann Smith, *Palestine and the Palestinians, 1876–1983* (1984); Charles D. Smith, *Palestine and the Arab-Israeli Conflict*, 4th ed. (2001); Mark Tessler, *A History of the Israeli-Palestinian Conflict* (1994); and Ian J. Bickerton and Carla L. Klausner, *A Concise History of the Arab-Israeli Conflict*, 3rd ed. (1998).

The period of the British mandate is covered by Tarif Khalidi, "Palestinian Historiography: 1900–1948," *Journal of Palestine Studies*, 10(3):59–76 (Spring 1981); Adnan Mohammed Abu-Ghazaleh, *Arab Cultural Nationalism in Palestine During the British Mandate* (1973); Sami Hadawi, *Bitter Harvest: A Modern History of Palestine*, 4th rev. and updated ed. (1991); Ann Mosely Lesch, *Arab Politics in Palestine, 1917–1939: The Frustration of a Nationalist Movement* (1979); Y. Porath, *The Emergence of the Palestinian-Arab National Movement, 1918–1929*, trans. from Hebrew (1974), and *The Palestinian Arab National Movement: From Riots to Rebellion, 1929–1939*, trans. from Hebrew (1977); Kenneth W. Stein, *The Land Question in Palestine, 1917–1939* (1984); Benny Morris, *The Birth of the Palestinian Refugee Problem, 1947–1949* (1987); Issa Khalaf, *Politics in Palestine: Arab Factionalism and Social Disintegration, 1939–1948*, (1991); Avi Shlaim, *Collusion Across the Jordan: King Abdullah, the Zionist Movement, and the Partition of Palestine* (1988), also published in a rev. abridged ed. as *The Politics of Partition: King Abdullah, the Zionists, and Palestine, 1921–1951* (1998); and Wm. Roger Louis and Robert W. Stookey (eds.), *The End of the Palestine Mandate* (1985).

Among the many studies on the Palestinian Arabs from 1948 to the present, the following are particularly worth consulting: Rashid Khalidi, *Palestinian Identity: The Construction of Modern National Consciousness* (1997); Helena

Cobban, *The Palestinian Liberation Organisation: People, Power, and Politics* (1984); F. Robert Hunter, *The Palestinian Uprising: A War by Other Means*, rev. and expanded ed. (1993); Ann Mosely Lesch, *Transition to Palestinian Self-Government* (1992); Shaul Mishal, *The PLO Under 'Arafat: Between Gun and Olive Branch* (1986); Don Peretz, *The West Bank: History, Politics, Society, and Economy* (1986), and *Intifada: The Palestinian Uprising* (1990); Julie M. Peteet, *Gender in Crisis: Women and the Palestinian Resistance Movement* (1991); Laurie A. Brand, *Palestinians in the Arab World: Institution Building and the Search for State* (1988); Barry Rubin, *The Arab States and the Palestine Conflict* (1981); Edward W. Said and Jean Mohr, *After the Last Sky: Palestinian Lives* (1986, reissued 1999); Ze'ev Schiff and Ehud Ya'ari, *Intifada: The Palestinian Uprising—Israel's Third Front*, ed. and trans. by Ina Friedman (1991; originally published in Hebrew, 1990); and Elia T. Zureik, *The Palestinians in Israel: A Study in Internal Colonialism* (1979).

Israel's physical and human geography are described in Efraim Orni and Elisha Efrat, *Geography of Israel*, 4th rev. ed. (1980). Studies in historical geography include Ruth Kark (ed.), *The Land That Became Israel* (1989); and Elisha Efrat, *Geography and Politics in Israel Since 1967* (1988). Leo Picard, *Structure and Evolution of Palestine: With Comparative Notes on Neighbouring Countries* (1943, reprinted 1959), is an authoritative and comprehensive geologic study. Michael Zohary, *Plant Life of Palestine: Israel and Jordan* (1962), is a fundamental work; and F.S. Bodenheimer, *Animal Life in Palestine: An Introduction to the Problems of Animal Ecology and Zoogeography* is a classic work on Israel's fauna. Settlements are discussed in Aharon Kellerman, *Society and Settlement: Jewish Land of Israel in the Twentieth Century* (1993).

Economic studies of Israel include Nadav Halevi and Ruth Klinov-Malul, *The Economic Development of*

Israel (1968); Yoram Ben-Porath (ed.), *The Israeli Economy: Maturing Through Crises* (1986); and, for more recent events, Yair Aharoni, *The Israeli Economy: Dreams and Realities* (1991); and Yakir Plessner, *The Political Economy of Israel: From Ideology to Stagnation* (1994). Administrative and political issues are explored by Don Peretz and Gideon Doron, *The Government and Politics of Israel*, 3rd ed. (1997); Alan Dowty, *The Jewish State: A Century Later* (1998); Yael Yishai, *Land of Paradoxes: Interest Politics in Israel* (1991); Gregory S. Mahler, *Israel: Government and Politics in a Maturing State* (1990); and Gregory S. Mahler (ed.), *Israel* (2000). Adam Garfinkle, *Politics and Society in Modern Israel*, 2nd ed. (2000), gives an excellent account of the interplay of Israel's domestic and foreign policy. Asher Arian (Alan Arian), *The Second Republic: Politics in Israel* (1998; originally published in Hebrew, 1997), is based on unique electoral demographic data.

Calvin Goldscheider, *Israel's Changing Society: Population, Ethnicity, and Development* (1996), is a useful work on demography and social structure. Sociological studies that summarize the great changes in Israeli life since independence include: Amir Ben-Porat, *Divided We Stand: Class Structure in Israel from 1948 to the 1980s* (1989); Eliezer Ben-Rafael and Stephen Sharot, *Ethnicity, Religion, and Class in Israeli Society* (1991); Gabriel Ben-Dor (ed.), *Israel in Transition* (1998); Dan Horowitz and Moshe Lissak, *Trouble in Utopia* (1989); and Baruch Kimmerling, *The Invention and Decline of Israeliness: Society, Culture and the Military*, (2001). Israeli culture is critically analyzed by Avishai Margalit, *Views in Review: Politics and Culture in the State of the Jews* (1998); and Ella Shohat, *Israeli Cinema: East/West and the Politics of Representation* (1989).

Works describing the Zionist movement and the establishment and subsequent history of Israel include Nahum Sokolow, *History of Zionism, 1600–1918*, 2 vol.

(1919, reprinted 2 vol. in 1, 1969); Leonard Stein, *Zionism* (1925, reissued 1932); Norman Bentwich, *Palestine* (1934, reissued 1946); Albert M. Hyamson, *Palestine Under the Mandate, 1920–1948* (1950, reprinted 1976); and Barnet Litvinoff, *To the House of Their Fathers: A History of Zionism* (1965). Valuable interpretations are contained in Peter Y. Medding, *The Founding of Israeli Democracy, 1948–1967* (1990); and Laurence J. Silberstein, *New Perspectives on Israeli History: The Early Years of the State* (1991).

The literature on Israel's history since 1948 is both vast and heated. Useful works include the admirably concise T.G. Fraser, *The Arab-Israeli Conflict* (1995); Conor Cruise O'Brien, *The Siege: The Saga of Israel and Zionism* (1986, reissued 1988); Bernard Reich et al. (eds.), *An Historical Encyclopedia of the Arab-Israeli Conflict* (1996); and Howard M. Sachar, *A History of Israel: From the Rise of Zionism to Our Times*, 2nd ed., rev. and updated (1996). Benny Morris, *Righteous Victory: A History of the Zionist-Arab Conflict, 1881–1999* (1999), is a good example of the controversial "new historians" school; and Martin Gilbert, *Atlas of the Arab-Israeli Conflict*, 6th ed. (also published as *The Dent Atlas of the Arab-Israeli Conflict*, 1993), provides critical geographic context.

Autobiographies of Israel's leaders reflect strong views and include David Ben-Gurion, *Israel: A Personal History* (1971, originally published in Hebrew, 1969); Menachem Begin, *The Revolt*, rev. ed. (1977, reissued 1983; originally published in Hebrew, 1950); Yigal Allon, *The Making of Israel's Army* (1970); Moshe Dayan, *Breakthrough: A Personal Account of the Egypt-Israel Peace Negotiations* (1981); and Golda Meir, *My Life* (1975, reissued 1977). Yitzhak Rabin, *The Rabin Memoirs*, expanded ed. (1996; originally published in Hebrew, 1979), should be supplemented by David Horovitz, *Shalom, Friend: The Life and Legacy of Yitzhak Rabin* (1996).

Palestinian autonomy is discussed in Harvey Sicherman, *Palestinian Self-Government (Autonomy): Its Past and Its Future* (1991; also published as *Palestinian Autonomy, Self-Government & Peace*, 1993); and an analysis of events within the Israel-Lebanon-Syria triangle is Moshe Ma'oz, *Syria and Israel: From War to Peacemaking* (1995). The monographic literature concerning Israel's important relationship with the United States includes William B. Quandt, *Peace Process: American Diplomacy and the Arab-Israeli Conflict Since 1967* (1993); and Bernard Reich, *Securing the Covenant: United States-Israel Relations After the Cold War* (1995). Dov S. Zakheim, *Flight of the Lavi* (1996), opens the window on the vital U.S.-Israeli military relationship. Finally, good accounts of Israel's peace diplomacy include David Makovsky, *Making Peace with the PLO: The Rabin Government's Road to the Oslo Accord* (1996); Itamar Rabinovitch, *The Brink of Peace: The Israeli-Syrian Negotiations* (1998); and Uri Savir, *The Process: 1,100 Days That Changed the Middle East* (1998).

INDEX

Palestinian self-rule in,
100–101, 102, 205
settlement of Israelis in, 88–89,
93, 102, 179, 181, 186, 189
Western Wall, 55, 130–131, 161,
168, 198
World War I and postwar period,
47–51, 108, 154–156
World War II and postwar
period, 62–67, 108, 156, 157
Wye River Memorandum,
199–200
Wye II, 201

Y

Yarqon River, 107–108
Yom Kippur War, 83, 173–176, 181

Z

Zionism, 46, 50, 52–54, 55, 56, 57,
60, 61–62, 63, 66, 67–69, 70,
138, 152, 153, 154–155, 156–
160, 162, 163, 167, 175, 177
opposition to, 47, 50, 51, 56,
64–65, 82, 93, 176